STEVE McQUEEN

A PASSION FOR SPEED

TEXT BY FRÉDÉRIC BRUN

EDITED BY YANN-BRICE DHERBIER

ENGLISH TRANSLATION FLO BRUTTON

STEVE McQUEEN

McQUEEN

A PASSION FOR SPEED

Text by Frédéric Brun

McQUEEN
A PASSION FOR SPEED

Text by Frédéric Brun

INTRODUCTION

America in the 1950s and 1960s was obsessed with modernity, and its dreams were fired by images of propulsion—whether that speed was delivered by an F-86 Sabre Jet, a Gemini rocket, or a blazing red Corvette. Steve McQueen was one of Hollywood's most popular actors, and he rode the wave of this machine-driven mania. Speed was at the heart of the McQueen mystique, a crucial dimension of his reputation as the "King of Cool." Speed raced him past other stars and defined his career. His prowess as a stunt driver, the awesome machines that he drove on screen, the motorcycles, planes, and cars that he drove in his off-screen life—these were the things that helped propel his fame so far and so wide. Without them, whatever his personal charisma, he would never have achieved such cult status.

The wicked grin, the piercing blue eyes—they said it all. Under his clothes, solid muscles. McQueen had the same discrete power as his sinewy speed machines. A man of few words but huge presence—that was his style. Quiet on the outside, complex on the inside. Right from the start, he displayed a taciturn nature that didn't always go down well on set. But he quickly saw how to turn that to his advantage. As he would later confide to Yul Brynner in the filming of *The Magnificent Seven*: Spacing out his lines was a clever way to garner more screen time.

Terrence Steven McQueen learned to bend the rules at an early age. Born on March 24, 1930, in Beech Grove, Indiana, he was abandoned by his father and spent a lonely, impoverished childhood with his often-battered mother and her succession of abusive partners. "My life," he often said, "was screwed up before I was born."

He was a turbulent, aggressive teenager who hung out with the Indianapolis gangs more than he hung out at school. He never made any secret of it: "When a kid didn't have any love when he was small, he begins to wonder if he's good enough. You know, if my mother didn't love me, and I didn't have a father, I mean, well, I guess I'm not very good. I've done everything that there is to do. I always did the things that other people wouldn't do. Some dangerous things. I never thought of myself as a particularly courageous person. I was always kind of a coward, constantly trying to prove myself."

In 1944 at the age of 14, he wound up in reform school. Two years later, draped over a bar early one morning, he signed up for the Merchant Marine. Next stop, Trinidad and the Dominican Republic, but not for long. Soon tired of the perfumed isles, he was off at the earliest opportunity, first to Canada and the joys of lumberjacking and then to North Carolina. Barroom brawling was a waste of his talents, so he thought to make some money fighting and signed up as a boxer. He then joined the United States Marines in 1947, where he served as a mechanic for three years, a tough preparation for his future role as a machinist's mate in *The Sand Pebbles*. McQueen wasn't just acting the part in that film. The scene when he whispers sweet nothings to the steam engine to get it started again—that scene says a lot.

The Marines brought McQueen his first experience of real friendship. With his irreverent, sardonic sense of humor and talent for imitating other people, McQueen was amusing company—apart from the time he spent in the brig for insubordinate behavior. His military career saw more work details than action, but did have its moment of glory when he saved the lives of five other Marines during a training exercise. McQueen was honorably discharged from the Marines in 1950.

So then what? Encyclopedia salesman, newspaper delivery boy, TV repairman, bookie, florist, taxi driver, truck driver, part-time mechanic in a motorcycle shop that serviced James Dean's machine—you name it, McQueen did it. But what he loved was driving. His only pastime in the 1950s was motorcycle racing, where he quickly made a name for himself. Motorcycles were his first and most enduring passion. However distinguished his career as an amateur racing driver, it was on two wheels—enduro and off-road— that he really excelled.

In 1955, McQueen was accepted to The Actors Studio. Bad-boy anti-heroes were then all the rage. McQueen debuted on Broadway that same year and moved into motion pictures in 1956, playing a bit part in *Somebody Up There Likes Me*, a boxer biopic starring Paul Newman.

And so began a new and more stable life, starting in 1956 with his marriage to actress Neile Adams. She bore him two children, Terry and Chad. Steve was starting to become known. In 1959, he played opposite Frank Sinatra in John Sturges' film *Never So Few*. Ol' Blue Eyes took an avuncular approach to his rebellious, scene-stealing young co-star. McQueen also landed the role that was to make him a household name in the TV series *Wanted: Dead or Alive*. McQueen played Josh Randall, an anti-hero bounty hunter always ready to take the law into his own hands.

The following year John Sturges signed him up again, this time for *The Magnificent Seven*. In 1963, he offered McQueen the leading role in *The Great Escape*. McQueen turned in a gripping performance as the irrepressible, scrappy officer who is determined to escape at any cost. The action scenes are impressive, complete with motorcycle stunts, many executed by the actor himself. And so it was that the McQueen style exploded onto the big screen, a mixture of the masterful and the laid-back, the reserved and the virile. The media loved him and christened him the "King of Cool." A superstar was born.

By the early 1970s, McQueen was the highest-paid actor in Hollywood, billed ahead of some of the greatest names in cinema. When he wasn't filming, he was racing, feeding his passion for speed and competition with powerful machines that he drove with considerable skill. The film *Le Mans* echoes his achievements in the 1970 12 Hours of Sebring at the wheel of a Porsche 908. The closer you look, the more the line between filmography and autobiography becomes blurred—very revealing in psychoanalytical terms.

Cinema often mirrored McQueen's real life. Looking back, we get a terrific—albeit distorted—insight into the man behind the legend by comparing the roles he played with his personality off screen. In real life, McQueen wasn't always a hero. He had a reputation as a quick-tempered actor who was unstable on set and prone to violent outbursts of insecurity. Married three times, he was twice divorced, first from Neile Adams on March 14, 1972, then from his second wife, actress Ali MacGraw, in 1978. The couple met on the set of *The Getaways* and married a year later on July 13, 1973. McQueen's third and final wife was Barbara Minty, a young model 17 years his junior whom he married on January 16, 1980. McQueen was a drug user, though he was never arrested. His attempts at rehab always ended in relapse due to his temper.

But his heart was ever in the right place. It was part of most film deals that he should get a supply of free items from the studio—electric razors, jeans, T-shirts—that he would then quietly donate to the Boys Republic Reform School, where he had spent time as a teenager.

McQueen's constant quest for identity made him very careful about his appearance and personal style. He collected fine watches with the discerning eye of a man who admired mechanical precision. His image today is linked to the Heuer Monaco chronograph (with the unmistakable square dial visible under the sleeve of the driver's suit that he wears in *Le Mans*). But for everyday wear, he had a perverse preference for delicate, elegant wristwatches and intricately complicated timepieces. Nothing flashy, mind you, and always high performance. His biker jackets and jeans, despite their apparent casualness, were in fact always adjusted to fit by his tailor.

In the making of *The Thomas Crown Affair* (which, he liked to point out, was the only film in which he wore a suit), he took great pleasure in personally assembling an ultra-chic wardrobe for the character. Tailor-made shirts, Cartier Tank Américaine wristwatch, and an umbrella with a long handle in precious wood. Thus attired, our world-weary gentlemen thief pursues his quest for inner peace, at the wheel of his Rolls-Royce coupé and living dangerously at the controls of his glider.

Steve McQueen the actor, the insatiable and complex King of Cool, attracted legions of fans at a very emotional level. Despite an uneven filmography that veers from blockbusters (*The Towering Inferno*) to classics (*Papillon* and *An Enemy of the People*) to other more pedestrian productions, McQueen was in everything the expression of an ambiguous, disconcerting personality—a character that everyone found incredibly seductive. Loved by women and admired by men, he built his reputation on sheer personal popularity.

Every daredevil must eventually pay the price. Nemesis, spirit of vengeance, always comes calling. For McQueen she took the form of cancer. He died on November 7, 1980, in a clinic in Juarez, Mexico, after receiving controversial experimental treatment. All of America mourned—probably because the characters he played, though rebellious, were always anchored in the conventional American values of his time. From reform school to success-ful racing driver and high-paid Hollywood star, Steve McQueen embodied numerous aspects of the American dream. And that dream was very much machine driven.

A PASSION FOR MACHINES

Steve McQueen's tastes spoke directly to the collective imagination of his time. His on-screen presence fulfilled every American's fantasies. He himself couldn't account for his popularity, but thought that maybe because he was an average Joe, people could identify with him. Maybe it also had something to do with his intrepid handling of racing machines—and because he personified the archetypal, freedom-loving, speed-loving tough-guy of the mid-twentieth century. Is it any wonder that the lead character in the animated movie *Cars* is called "Lightning McQueen"?

McQueen's garage always held an array of fast cars and motorcycles. He once told an interviewer that he attributed his interest in racing to his great-uncle Claude and the red tricycle he got for his fourth birthday.

One of the first things he did when he moved to New York in 1952 was buy a sports car: an English MG TC, bought for $450 in a suburb of Columbus, Ohio. The little car provided some exhilarating experiences, but suffered badly at the hands of its driver. After the rear axle broke for the third time, McQueen got rid of it and turned to motorcycles. He meanwhile did whatever he could to earn a living, displaying a flair for all things mechanical that occasionally got him work in a local repair shop. It wasn't until he moved to California and married actress Neile Adams that he regained his interest in cars. First came a sleek and stylish Austin-Healey, then a red Corvette with white coves. Wife Neile, meanwhile, didn't think much of Steve's machines—and thought even less of them after she had an accident in the Corvette. So just for her sake, Steve bought a quiet, well-behaved white Ford Fairlane convertible.

Motorcycles were his consolation on weekends. A seasoned amateur racer even back then (before the sport really caught on), he would spend hours race-tuning his machine. The sitting room carpet did double duty as his workshop. Too bad about the oil spills—being machine-proud was more important than being house-proud. The first thing he did on returning from a race was clean the machine for its next event. Showering for dinner came second.

McQueen would own all sorts of motorcycles: competition-class, motocross, on-road, and off-road. They included, of course, a Triumph Bonneville and TR6SC ISDT, as well as a Husqvarna 400 CR, Indian Chief, and Norton, plus quite a few antique motorcycles from the 1920s and earlier that he began collecting in the 1970s. Not forgetting his Solex 3800 motorized bicycle—great fun on the *Le Mans* set.

By 1957, McQueen was itching for another sports car. First came a Siata 208, then a Porsche 356 Speedster followed by a Lotus XI and a very rare Jaguar XK-SS. For his 34th birthday his wife Neille gave him a superb Ferrari 250 GT Lusso. Sometime later he got the chance to drive another Ferrari, the uniquely elegant convertible 275 GTS/4 NART. By 1969, he was back behind the wheel of a Porsche, starting with a 911S, soon followed by a 911 Turbo, and ultimately a 930. As a racing driver, Steve McQueen drove some of the most desirable machines of his time. After making his debut in the Porsche 356 and the Lotus, he raced a Cooper T52 Formula Junior, an Austin-Healey Sprite Sebring, a Porsche 908, and a Porsche 917. He also drove the desert in a Vic Hickey–designed Hurst Baja Boot racing buggy. Over the years, McQueen stabled beasts of every description: a Mini Cooper S (stardom oblige), a VW Beetle, Mustang, and Corvette; a Chevy V-8-powered Jeep and Land Rover; and a whole fleet of pickups (GMC, Chevy, Ford) to patrol his properties in Santa Paula, California, and Ketchum, Idaho. The lineup also included a sleek, full-size Cadillac Sedan, a 1957 Chevrolet Bel Air convertible, a Hudson Wasp Coupe, a Cadillac Series 62, an Excalibur, a Mercedes-Benz 280 SE 3.5, and a Mercedes-Benz 300 SEL 6.3 (his favorite full-size sedan, though he did have a brief fling with a Rolls-Royce Corniche Cabrio).

Then there were all the machines he drove on the big screen, from the mocked-up German military motorcycle in *The Great Escape* (actually a disguised Triumph) to the Corvair-powered dune buggy he had built for *The Thomas Crown Affair*. And who could forget the 1968 Mustang GT Fastback pursuing the Dodge Charger in the iconic *Bullitt* car chase or the Porsche 917 featured in *Le Mans*?

As one might expect, it was not chance or fashion alone that got these machines their parts in a full-length movie. McQueen himself had a hand in it, as much for his own enjoyment as for that of his fans. His love of mechanical things was contagious, and he communicated it in print media too. The August 1966 issue of *Sports Illustrated* magazine features his review of eight of the fastest cars of the time: the Aston Martin DB6, Jaguar E type 2+2, Mercedes 230 SL, Alfa Romeo Duetto Spider, Ferrari 275 GTS, Porsche 911, Corvette, and the Shelby Cobra 427. Titled "A Star Among Fast Friends," the feature shows him on the race course at Riverside, near Los Angeles—Hollywood star and championship racer on two wheels and four now turned sports writer.

A MAN OF HIS TIME

Freud said the human male's most powerful sex organ is his brain. The same might be said of driving motorcars and other vehicles: speed isn't just thrills, spills, and heart-pounding euphoria. It has an intellectual and visceral aspect that in the twentieth century invaded the world of the visual arts—from Bolidismo and Pop Art to the "Art Cars" prepared for the 24 Hours of Le Mans.

You get the feeling of speed at the wheel of a sports car. French writer Françoise Sagan said that private car ownership would give master and servant alike the paradoxical impression of being free at last. For postwar man, the motorcar was more than a pleasure. It was his ticket to twentieth-century heaven.

Into this steps Steve McQueen, a modern-day knight come to deliver postwar America from the stranglehold of crowded highways choked with trucks and chrome-clad sedans. Built under Franklin Roosevelt's New Deal, these two-lane highways had become a caricature of their former glory. The gleaming interstate freeways of the 1960s were yet to come. American cities were strangled by thick traffic congestion. Speed was escape.

The visual arts at this time celebrated spontaneity—quick sketches, doodles, art in the raw, as it happens, untrammeled by formal convention. "Action painting," sometimes called "gestural abstraction," revolutionized American visual arts by putting creativity into motion. Jasper Johns and particularly Robert Rauschenberg launched a new artistic quest focused on the art object, bridging the gap between the generation of the great masters of abstract expressionism and Pop Art (that would also celebrate speed and the motorcar).

It is ever the role of contemporary artists to further social mobility and break down resistance to new ideas. Drawing from the culture of their age, they give shape to emerging trends in society. Art-meets-automobile was bound to happen sooner or later—not just making the motorcar the subject, but occasionally making it the work of art itself. The most famous examples of this were the "Art Cars" entered a decade later for the 24 Hours of Le Mans by the auctioneer and amateur racing driver Hervé Poulain. Art Cars were based on the concept of the "walk-in" mobile: a canvas that moves past the audience, as originally conceived in 1974 by artist Alexander Calder and subsequently interpreted by other artists including Roy Lichtenstein and Andy Warhol.

Speed had an effect not just on painting and the visual arts, but across the entire spectrum of artistic disciplines, music in particular. The many incarnations of jazz—from bebop to the free jazz championed by Robert Ayler, Charlie Mingus, and John Coltrane—gave free rein to improvisation in a constant quest for energy that produced experimental forms like hard bop and Miles Davis–style modal jazz.

Little by little, speed killed form. Energy got the better of matter. The thirst for freedom, progress, and movement reaped the whirlwind. Just as the oil lamp in the Hindu festival of Diwali symbolizes the victory of knowledge over ignorance, so the fast car of the twentieth century came to epitomize the triumph of technology over time—both examples of a fascinating process that begins when the spirit of the age becomes embodied in a person or thing. The fascination begins when the character or object comes to embody its time.

This was a time when highways were virtually non-existent in Europe. European air travel was a rarity, and train journeys were long and boring. Tightly controlled exchange rates placed foreign cars out of reach. The "sports car" was a fantasy object, unthinkably powerful, unthinkably fast, and exhilarating beyond belief. To handle such a vehicle (while others just drove) was to join an elite few. Steve McQueen, driven by a passion for speed, was the perfect embodiment of his age. His presence on the big screen, like James Dean 10 years earlier, was the perfect expression of America's changing relationship with time, distance, and freedom.

ADDICTED TO SPEED

To go fast was to transcend oneself, exceed one's limitations, and break free of inertia. Considered in this way, the craving for speed is easier to understand. "Racing," said McQueen, who knew a thing or two about recreational drugs, "is the most exciting thing there is. But unlike drugs, you get high with dignity." Everyone who raced with him or against him commented on his perfectionism, his painstaking preparation, and his ability to concentrate.

He knew, of course, that there was something obsessive and addictive about his love of racing. Maniacs like him, he used to say, listen to no one—as if just the sound of the engines made them high. But what racing also did, for sure, was bring him out of himself. As he once told journalists, speed was the ultimate panacea. "It's only when I'm going fast in a racing car or on a bike that I can really relax."

The scene in *The Thomas Crown Affair* when our hero skims the treetops to land his glider could be straight out of McQueen's real life. In the film, the woman waiting for him is horrified, but Crown shrugs it off, saying only that if he did crash then at least he wouldn't have to worry anymore. She fails to see what a man like him has to worry about. "Who I want to be tomorrow," says McQueen, alias Thomas Crown, with a wry smile and a twinkle in his eye.

"Frenetic speed," wrote Japanese philosopher Masaharu Anesaki in 1924 "is an expression of the spirit of rebellion, a state of conflict between inertia and motion." Pointing out that notions of speed are commonly paired with notions of progress, he added: "Speed is the visible demonstration of progress." Everything that Steve McQueen did, in the eyes of America and ultimately the entire world, would be marked by his drive for progress and modernity. But he did it by stepping outside the box, by competing against himself and others—no gloves, no niceties. "I enjoy racing in any form because the guy next to me couldn't care less what my name is. He just wants to beat me." McQueen proved himself by being daring, and that meant taking risks.

The specter of death looms over every racetrack. Chad McQueen has never forgotten the day back in 1970 when his father took him out on a motorcycle to see the mangled carcass of a wrecked car. It was on the set of *Le Mans*, and Chad was 10 years old. McQueen summoned him over and told his worried-looking little son that he was about to see what could happen in a race. Short, sharp, and to the point—a lesson as much for the teacher as for his student. Extreme strength meets fatal weakness.

THE SHADOW OF DANGER

Taking command of a powerful machine is the racing driver's route to freedom. But for all the thrill of the chase, lurking around every bend is the prospect of the crash—the gamble that didn't pay off.

Accidents, until very recently, were as much a part of car driving as speed, mainly because cars and roads alike were only more or less reliable. French poet and academician Jean Cocteau professed an aversion to both, appalled by what he describes in *La Machine Infernale* as "the horror that hits you when you come across a road accident, struck by the stillness of speed and the scream turned silent." The 1950s and 1960s would prove him cruelly right, as celebrity after celebrity came to grief on the road.

The first famous case was James Dean, symbol of a rise to stardom that was brutally cut short. On September 30, 1956, Dean set off for a car race at the wheel of his silver Porsche 550 Spyder, which he nicknamed *Little Bastard*. With him was his favorite mechanic, Rolf Wüterich. In the days prior to the trip, fellow actor Alec Guinness expressed a bad feeling about the car. Three hours into the journey, at the junction of highways 466 and 41 near the small town of Cholame, California, a Ford Tutor failed to yield to the oncoming Porsche. Its driver, a distracted Cal-Poly student called Donald Turnupseed, made an illegal left turn. The two cars collided. Of the three men involved in the crash, only Dean was killed. He had just completed the final scene for *Giant*, directed by George Stevens, with co-star Elizabeth Taylor. In a final twist of fate, Dean's studio contract expressly forbade him from driving fast or entering any race while the film was being made. News of his death stunned the world.

The next victim, six months later, was French novelist Françoise Sagan. Driving down a country road at speeds over 175 kilometers per hour (100 miles per hour), she lost control of her Aston Martin DB 2/4. The car skidded violently, flipped twice, and trapped its slender driver under nearly two tons of steel. It was a horrific accident, and for many days, Sagan hovered between life and death. The press held its breath, as did the whole of France. Françoise Sagan was given the last rites and pumped full of drugs; she survived but would remain a lifelong addict. For Sagan, speed was a game of chance between the driver and death: gambling for high stakes was what made it so exhilarating. "Whoever has not thrilled to speed has not thrilled to life," she wrote. "Speed is no sign, no proof, no provocation, no challenge, but rather a surge of happiness."

There is something supremely fateful about car accidents. They are the modern-day trial by ordeal: a confrontation with death that bestows superhuman status. The racing driver, like the gladiator in the arena or the matador in the bullring, looks death in the eye and fights it with his bare hands. If he wins, or at least survives, he becomes a hero like Juan Manuel Fangio or Niki Lauda. If he loses, his legend is forever altered. Alberto Ascari, Alfonso de Portago, Porfirio Rubirosa, and later Ayrton Senna are good examples. As a seasoned racing driver, Steve McQueen had learned to deal with danger but he could not learn to overcome it—in motor racing, the risks are inevitably beyond control.

THE PRICE OF COMMITMENT

Steve McQueen spent his life chasing happiness. Motorcycles, cars, and airplanes were his ticket to ride, his passport out of his unhappy past to somewhere altogether different. But getting there required a huge investment of time and money, physical and mental discipline.

Racing drivers must be in top physical shape and capable of enormous concentration. Watching the film *Le Mans*, you get a cockpit view of what it feels like to be the person behind the wheel: the nervous tension, the fatigue, the rush of adrenaline, and heart-pounding acceleration. But what you don't feel is the temperature inside the cockpit. Caged in metal and glass, a sports-prototype cockpit is a furnace. Racecars are stripped of all unnecessary weight, including insulation, and the cockpit grows increasingly hot. The temperature inside that little cabin can easily soar past 120 degrees Fahrenheit, putting the driver under extreme physical and mental stress. Other problems include hunger, but mainly thirst and excessive sweating, both aggravated by the driver's flame-retardant suit, balaclava, helmet, boots, and gloves. As night falls on the 24-hour track, the hurtling machines become incandescent. Asthenopia, the technical name for acute eyestrain, now joins the other challenges of high-speed driving. Wherever they may finish, drivers reach the finish line exhausted.

For a racer, a well-tuned body is at least as important as a well-tuned machine. Steve McQueen was one of the first Hollywood stars to pay attention to his physique and not just because he was image-conscious; he knew his body was his greatest ally when it came to doing the things he loved most: racing cars. He was a perfectionist to the core, with an iron discipline that occasionally extended to his family and friends. He was also a man of contradictions, with a punishing exercise regime and an equally punishing addiction to cigarettes and other recreational drugs. But to judge from the pictures of Steve McQueen in command of a sports car, airplane, or motorbike, he obviously enjoyed his commitment. He loved what he did and his enthusiasm was contagious. It was a game of seduction to which he was prepared to devote a huge amount time.

A game of seduction is also how French novelist Michel Déon describes the love of cars in his memoir: "Cars were my dancing girls. For their sake, I stood around freezing in filthy garages, envying the greasy hands that fiddled with their private parts. I loved giving them a bath, polishing their soft surfaces with special creams, raising and lowering their tops and showering them with little jewels—mirrors, headlights, radiator caps. On long night journeys, I would stop on a minor road and sleep inside them, all passion spent, my cheek pressed against their leather cushions. Dawn would wake us, stirring us to make love all over again." Such intense, carnal eagerness can only be understood in the context of those times.

What has become of those dreams of seduction, performance, and progress? Today, the car has fallen from grace. Once regarded as an instrument of freedom and creative thinking of the most fascinating kind, the car is now the bête noire of environmentalists and safety campaigners. Today's cars all look the same, manufactured by standard production methods and fitted with electronic driving aids that remove the onus of responsibility from the driver. The stallion has been tamed, reined in by the vice-like grip of driving regulations. Slowly but surely, rather than try to master danger, we have done away with notions of risk altogether. Precaution has been elevated to dogma and the dream has by stages been brought to reason.

These days, those dreams of Steve McQueen and his machines are strictly for nostalgia junkies and chivalrous romantics. He once said that speed was his *raison d'être*, his lifeline, the girl to whom he gave his all, in the knowledge that she would never betray him. Those freedoms he so cherished as an actor would be hard to find today, undermined by the media, studios and agents, in a climate of opinion that only tolerates excess with moderation. Speed has the taste of forbidden fruit; the effect of a powerful stimulant, an unstable force set to destroy whoever consumes it.

It is this that makes Steve McQueen so dangerously irresistible. It no doubt also explains why, after all these decades, the life and loves of Steve McQueen are the admiration of a new generation that never saw his films on the big screen. McQueen had momentum, he brought hope of a freedom that any might grasp, a happiness that was there for the taking. Today he is the icon of a golden age long gone, worshipped by people hungry for nostalgia. In that respect at least, he still represents the spirit of the rebel who resists the conformist agenda of his times. And the more conventional our society becomes, the more attractive that image looks.

Steve McQueen's shattered destiny, cut off in his prime, is a powerful testament to the immobility of death and the movement of life.

McQUEEN

THE PURSUIT OF SPEED

McQUEEN
THE PURSUIT OF SPEED

MCQUEEN THE PURSUIT OF SPEED

Le Mans, Sebring, Brands Hatch, Riverside—Steve McQueen would one day compete on all of these tracks. But to find the place where it all started we have to head to Slater, Missouri, where he lived as a boy on his great-uncle Claude's farm. It was here on the hill overlooking the farm that McQueen discovered his passion for competition and speed.

Claude Thomson was a gruff but kindly man. He treated his great-nephew like his own son and introduced him to the joys of the great outdoors. McQueen's first ever "machine," the vehicle that taught him the thrill of the chase, was a red tricycle, a present for his fourth birthday. Steve McQueen, future championship racer on two and four wheels, made his debut on three. Not content to fly down the hill on his own, the little boy started to organize races with other kids. Where they came from didn't matter. What counted was beating them and winning (usually candy). McQueen often came first, which gave him some satisfaction, but mainly lots of fun.

The die was cast. McQueen would never lose his competitive spirit, pitting himself against the best in the world. "I enjoy racing in any form because the guy next to me couldn't care less what my name is. He just wants to beat me." Taking on others also brought him out of himself, forcing him to confront his own doubts.

Intrepid, impulsive, perfectionist, always in great physical shape—McQueen would make a great racing driver. Plus he was a fighter. People who met him through racing said he was one of the most focused and unassuming guys in the paddock. He knew his limitations and was aware that he was an amateur among professionals. As a highly tuned athlete, he had plenty of stamina and endurance, but as a racing driver, he could be too impetuous—his line sometimes lacked refinement, and he tended to overwork the engine. He would never have the precision skills required for Formula 1, and he knew it. But he was well respected by his friends and fellow competitors.

Bitten by the racing bug, McQueen dreamed of being a racing driver. Two wheels or four, it didn't matter. "I don't know if I'm an actor who races or a racer who acts," he once told William Nolan. He was only half joking, because in the end he never would take the plunge, never abandon a movie career that did even more for his sense of achievement than it did for his bank account. But racing was his opportunity for catharsis: high on speed, he left his hang-ups behind.

He competed in countless events, turning in commanding performances aboard a motorcycle or at the wheel of an automobile,

with a few memorable dates along the way. As a young actor in 1958, he acquired a 1958 Porsche 356 1600 Super Speedster. It was his first brand-new car—and the first thing he did was strip it of everything he thought unnecessary on a racing machine, from the lightweight bumper and decorative chrome-plated accessories right down to the little Reutter coach builder badge. Fitted with minimal windscreen and Rudge alloy knock-off wheels, the Speedster was ready to hit the track.

"No frills" car, "no frills" kit: just a minimal helmet with leather chinstrap, aviator-style goggles, cotton biker jacket, and T-shirt. Thus kitted out and with a number of events already under his belt, McQueen competed at the Riverside International Raceway, a popular track in Southern California. First time at Riverside, first time lucky. But he was still just a beginner, passionate and raring to go, but too impetuous and with a lot to learn. He was a great believer in the principle that practice makes perfect. "Each time you race, you learn more," was his motto. What he learned to begin with, he taught himself. What he learned later, he learned from the best.

After the Porsche 356 came a Lotus Eleven (AKA the Lotus XI or Lotus 11)—a fascinating speed machine if ever there was one: svelte, ground-hugging, and stunningly streamlined, with super-aerodynamic bodywork. Descended from the Lotus Mk IX, the Lotus Eleven combined a thin-gauge aluminum body with a tubular space-frame chassis. It was British-made and came in three basic models to suit a connoisseur market of racing drivers, racing stables, and gentlemen drivers. The "Le Mans" was mainly for competition use, with de Dion rear axle. The "Club" had a live rear axle. The "Sport" was similar to the Club but with a more powerful engine. The sportiest models had Girling disc brakes on all four wheels; the rest made do with drum brakes. Weighing no more than 992 pounds, the Lotus Eleven topped the 100-horsepower mark. There was also a road version equipped with a cheaper Ford 100E 1172 side-valve engine, producing just 36 horsepower—no aerodynamic head fairing, but it had a windscreen and washers.

Gentlemen drivers obviously preferred the sportier models, particularly since the Lotus Eleven was equipped for road and track (with indicators, parking lights, and high- and low-beam headlights) so could be driven to the event on public roads. For the Sunday racing driver—a popular breed in Britain after World War II—it couldn't have been easier. He packed his tweed jacket in an overnight bag, donned bomber jacket, string-backed gloves, motorcycle helmet, and goggles, and drove straight to the starting line. At night, beaten or triumphant, he simply drove back the way

he had come. The Lotus in general, and the Eleven in particular, was made with him in mind.

This formidable motorcar was the ultimate expression of the principles pursued by its designer, Colin Chapman. Chapman was a visionary in his field who revolutionized race car design on the basis of a recipe that was also one of the best ever for sports leisure driving. Speed for Chapman was not just a matter of power. He sought performance by "adding lightness." This meant stripping away anything that might come between the driver and his vehicle and the road. Chapman's approach was innovative and also highly controversial, inviting as much trouble as success. But it positioned Lotus as one of the most radical race car constructors, in whatever category or event, whether Formula 1, the Indianapolis 500, Tour de France Automobile, or the 24 Hours of Le Mans.

In 1956 and 1957, the Lotus Eleven won the 1100cc class at Le Mans. The Eleven was Lotus' most emblematic model and what turned Lotus from a minor sports car constructor into the constructor that set the benchmark in Formula 1.

The Series 2 was launched in 1957 with a chassis reinforced to take the increased output from its more potent, 140-plus-horsepower engine. Steve McQueen's Lotus was a 1959 Lotus Sport Competition with an 1100cc Coventry Climax engine. "In that Lotus I really started to become competitive. I was smoother, more relaxed; the rough edges had been knocked off my driving. I was beginning to find out what real sports car racing was all about."

Labor Day weekend 1959, Santa Barbara. Saturday afternoon, Day One. It is the first time McQueen has raced in his Lotus and only his second real race. His car carries the number 33. Dressed in cotton overalls, driver's goggles slung around his neck and smoking a cigarette, he jumps into the tiny cockpit. Viewed from behind the fairing that crowned the riveted aluminum bodywork, he looks like a U.S. Air Force World War II ace about to take off for a mission over the Pacific. And he is quivering with impatience.

And they're off! Lap after agile lap, McQueen's Lotus makes mincemeat of the other cars, running rings around the big-engined American cars. Just five laps to go and the race's other Lotus Eleven closes in, engaging McQueen in a wheel-to-wheel battle for first position that sees him take a very respectable second. Everything looks good for the decisive race on Day Two. Sunday brings a repeat performance—same players, same results. McQueen and the other Lotus driver are soon elbow to elbow, their two Lotuses locked in combat. McQueen gets overconfident and tries to force his way past, nose to tail. He spins his car and stalls the engine. There are two cars in front of him by the time he's back in the running, and he finishes in fourth position. A humbling experience, but, as

he admits, that's what you get for being cocky. He swears it won't happen again—but it does. The 1959 season finishes at it started, with McQueen cursing his carelessness.

The occasion was the Del Mar event in California, McQueen's last Lotus engagement. It started well, with McQueen holding his lead for some time. But then he got careless. "I accidentally hit this switch on the dash which cut my power. It was an emergency fuel switch for changing tanks. As a result, the car just died on me." This was a moment of inattention that cost him the race. Furious, McQueen threw one of his famous temper tantrums. But he had learned his lesson and was now well on his way to becoming a real racing driver. A meeting with John Cooper would complete the job.

John Newton Cooper (1923–2000) was a born-and-bred craftsman. He was a thickset, broad-shouldered Englishman from Kingston in Surrey, with a genial personality and a great sense of humor. Cooper brought Formula 1 into the modern era by putting the engine behind the driver, challenging Enzo Ferrari's front-engined cars on Ferrari's home turf. Cooper also transformed Sir Alec Issigonis' classic, city-going Mini into that formidable racing machine, the Mini Cooper S, several times winner in the Monte Carlo Rally.

Cooper was the holder of several records at Montlhéry and well acquainted with the heady delights of speed and the allure of competition. After the war, with neither the money nor the quality materials he needed to compete on power, he opted for invention, which explains why his racing machines seem pretty rudimentary compared with those of the competition (especially the Transalps). But what they had going for them was lightness, ease of handling and simplicity. By putting his faith in McQueen, to the point of giving him a works car, Cooper fuelled his protégé's racing addiction—but he also gave it direction by passing on some of his own skills and technical savvy.

And so it was in 1962 that McQueen made his grand comeback to the paddock, two years after he was ordered off the track while making the TV series *Wanted: Dead or Alive*. As soon as the series was over, and fresh from shooting *The Magnificent Seven*, he was back behind the wheel—this time in a classy, elegant single-seater Cooper T52 Formula Junior. The CSI (International Sporting Commission) adopted the Formula Junior racing class in 1958. It was intended as an entry-level class that would safeguard the commercial viability of the tracks with a more accessible and therefore more competitive style of championship. It would give spectators a more varied program of events and reduce the costs for competitors. However, the class was short-lived, replaced in 1964 by Formula 3 (Formula 3 cars had standard engines; Formula 2 cars had competition engines).

The year before, starting in the fall, McQueen had spent quite some time in England shooting *The War Lover*. Great Britain back then was a real haven for lovers of sweet machines. Stirling Moss (one of McQueen's very few heroes) arranged for the newcomer to join the Cooper stable, racing under the wing of the BMC works team—the team that raced the Mini Cooper. Alongside him were people like Moss himself, Pedro Rodriguez, Innes Ireland—simply the best in the business. McQueen finally felt like one of the gang. And because he was a personable guy, he was invited to race on hallowed ground: the 12 Hours of Sebring in Florida.

The day before, as a warm-up, he competed in a three-hour event for production race cars. Driving his lightweight Austin-Healey Sebring Sprite, McQueen got a taste of uncharted territory, battling against the rain and up against stiff competition from a swarm of seasoned racing drivers. And for a beginner, albeit a smart one, he put in a very respectable performance, placing 9th out of 28. The following day, alongside fellow team member John Colgate (heir to the toothpaste dynasty), he held the lead for nearly seven hours at the wheel of his Austin-Healey 3000—a rare Le Mans fastback coupe. He eventually retired with engine failure, but it didn't matter. He'd done it. And he'd be back—with a vengeance.

His consolation in the meantime was to finish the season in style, entering as many local events as possible in his Cooper T52 Formula Junior. He was a noted success—at Del Mar, the Cotati Raceway, and the track that saw his first motor-racing exploits, Santa Barbara, where he now savored his last race of the season down to the very last drop. Three days later, he started filming *The Great Escape*. And that was it for racing. The studios gave him no choice. Only this time, he gave in gracefully. Waiting for him on the set was something guaranteed to keep him amused: the Triumph Bonneville motorcycle, his ticket to posterity thanks to some great stunts.

Hollywood knew just how to handle McQueen. The major film studios kept him busy on a continuous succession of shoots that meant he no longer had the time for car racing. So instead he raced motorcycles. Off-road in particular—short, sharp, and stomach-lurching—packed exactly his kind of kick. Amongst countless local and beginner events, his performance in the 1964 International Six Days Trial, with the United States team, was truly impressive. This was also when he discovered off-road desert racing, driving under the NORA banner. Thanks to fellow racers Bud and Dave Ekins, McQueen developed the same fascination for great desert expanses as he felt for the track.

The Stardust 7-11 on June 13 and 14, 1968, was his baptism by fire. It also marked a new addition to the McQueen stable. "Baja Boot" buggies—strange-looking custom-made four-wheel drives built by Vic Hickey—joined his collection of two- and four-wheel vehicles. The years 1967–1969 brought a string of successes, most notably at the notorious Baja 1000. McQueen raved about Hickey's machines, powering them through the heat and dust as if there were no tomorrow, a pleasure he would, of course, bring to the screen as gentleman-thief Thomas Crown at the wheel of a Meyers Manx dune buggy.

Despite the sharp attire of Thomas Crown, his favorite outfit would always be a racing suit. The one he wore for the magazine shoot of him and a magnificent Lola at Riverside Raceway, California, was light blue. With it went dark leather boots with white laces, blue Bell helmet with two metallic silver bands, big goggles, and a wrist stopwatch. His best-known outfit is probably the one he wore in *Le Mans*, sporting Gulf Oil colors. But the one that won him the most medals has to be the white one with his name embroidered on the right chest that he wore at the wheel of his Porsche 908 Spyder.

Solar Productions originally bought the Spyder for the movie *Day of the Champion*, which never went into production. It was a fantastic track car, entered by McQueen for three races, first at the difficult Holtville track (San Diego) in February 1970; next at Riverside; and lastly at Sebring in March 1970, for the 12 Hour classic that would prove the defining race of his career.

The 908 Spyder had a 350-horsepower, 3.0-liter flat eight engine and weighed just 640 kg (about 1,400 pounds), combining lightness with effective aerodynamic performance. The body shell was relatively tall—all that showed above the waistline was the driver's helmet and the rearview mirrors—and its long, flat lines earned it the nickname "flounder" or "sole." The bodywork started at ground level and finished with small, twin spoilers at the rear. McQueen's car was white.

McQueen always liked to surround himself with the best, and Sebring was no exception. For the record, the race was billed as a warm-up for the shooting of *Le Mans*. But off the record, McQueen fully expected to clinch a place, preferably one on the podium. And with that in mind, he teamed up with seasoned race driver Peter Revson, sporting the number 48.

Born in 1939 in New York City, Peter Revson was the son of cosmetics magnate Charles Revson, the man who gave the world indelible lipstick (launched under the Revlon brand—Revson swapped the "s" in his name for an "l" in honor of the chemist who came up with a kiss-proof formula for lipstick). One of McQueen's mechanics introduced him to Peter Revson, and the two men hit if off immediately. Honest and direct, Revson was McQueen's kind of guy.

Peter Revson made his motor-racing debut in the late 1950s. In 1964, he got his first Formula 1 ride in a Lotus-BRM and by 1966 had become one of endurance racing's biggest stars. In 1971, he drove his McLaren to victory in the Can-Am championship, also taking second place in the Indianapolis 500. In 1972, McLaren invited him back into the hallowed Formula 1 paddock. He remained with McLaren for two years, winning the British Grand Prix in 1973 followed by the Canadian edition later that season. Despite his outstanding performance, he was replaced in the McLaren team the following season by a rising star, Brazilian-born Emerson Fittipaldi. Revson, cast in the role of outsider, then moved to the Shadow team. On March 22, 1974, a week before the South African Grand Prix, he went to Kyalami near Johannesburg for a private testing session. He knew the track well and took a few risks. At full acceleration, the car suffered a suspension failure, and the ensuing crash killed Revson instantly. Steve McQueen attended his funeral. He rarely went in for shows of emotion, but the bonds between men on the same team or sharing the same car run deep . . . it is the same for drivers and mechanics alike.

Steve McQueen was always openly grateful to his mechanics and never more so than at the 12 Hours of Sebring in 1970. That year, he turned up at the track with a broken foot—legacy of a motorcycle racing accident the weekend before at the Elsinore Grand Prix. For Peter Revson, not surprisingly, this did not augur well for their prospects of glory—but he was forgetting just how determined McQueen could be. His mechanics used a thin strip of metal wrapped in leather and bound with adhesive tape to make him a makeshift splint—rigid enough to support his ankle but slim enough to fit inside his laced boot. That made two handicaps the Solar crew had to contend with: McQueen's physical disability and the Spyder's relative lack of power compared with the nearly 5-liter performance of the works cars they were up against—particularly the one driven by virtuoso racing driver Mario Andretti. But the McQueen/Revson crew drove an epic, truly stunning race, clinching a very honorable second place overall and winning first place in the 3-liter class.

McQueen was awarded the Hayden Williams Memorial Sportmanship trophy for his "incredible leg-in-a-cast driving performance." This trophy was sure to take a place of pride among the many displayed on his shelves—all tributes to the career of an amateur driver who was consumed by a burning passion for racing.

Previous page: Riverside Raceway, near Los Angeles. McQueen road tests a Ferrari 275 GTS (3.3-liter V-12 engine, priced then at $14,500), one of eight cars he reviewed for the August 1966 issue of *Sports Illustrated* magazine. Notable others included the Aston Martin DB6 (this page), Cobra 427 (facing page), and Lola T70 (pages 29 and 30). This Ferrari was his favorite. Verdict: "Wow," printed in bold. Best performance, best finish.

Above: The Aston Martin DB6, the most expensive of the eight tested (list price then, $15,500). Verdict: Great lines, luxurious interior, muscular performance, but disappointing acceleration in fifth gear.

The Cobra 427, featuring Ford's 7.0-liter V-8 engine ($7,495). Verdict: Fabulous acceleration, but disappointing handling, and driving position lacks comfort.

McQueen puts the Lola T70 through its paces at Riverside Raceway.

McQUEEN
DRIVES
PORSCHE

12 HOURS OF
SEBRING 1970
**Prototype winner
and 2nd overall
on Porsche 908**
HOLTVILLE RACE 1970
**Overall winner
on Porsche 908**
PHOENIX RACE 1970
**Overall winner
on Porsche 908**

Left: 1970s poster celebrating McQueen's wins at the wheel of a Porsche 908.

Above: The 1970 12 Hours of Sebring: McQueen and ex–Formula 1 racer Peter Revson in the Porsche 908 (Number 48) side by side with Jo Siffert in the Gulf Porsche 917K (Number 14). McQueen proved himself one to watch, overtaking Siffert, who was forced to pit with wheel-bearing problems.

McQueen and Revson fought their way through the pack to take second place overall, beaten to the checkered flag by Italian racing legend Mario Andretti driving a Ferrari 512S (Number 19). Andretti's other victories include the 1969 Indy 500, four IndyCar titles between 1965 and 1984, and the 1978 Formula 1 World Championship.

Left and above: California desert, 1961. McQueen and friend riding Triumph "desert sleds". McQueen was an excellent rider who as a student at The Actor's Studio survived between paychecks by racing his motorcycle.

Indian Dunes Race, 1970: McQueen (in the foreground) launches his Husqvarna from the starting line.

Sports Illustrated

AUGUST 23, 1971   60 CENTS

STEVE McQUEEN
ESCAPES
ON
Wheels

®

1963: McQueen prepares himself for a Mojave Desert race.

McQUEEN

THE BODY AS
TUNED MACHINE

McQUEEN
THE BODY AS TUNED MACHINE

MCQUEEN THE BODY AS TUNED MACHINE

For the racing driver, high-altitude pilot, or off-road rider, success never comes without painstaking preparation. The better the work at this stage, the safer, stronger, and more reliable the performance will be. McQueen was a stickler for preparation. The effort he devoted to machine maintenance and stunt practice was equaled only by his rigorous commitment to personal fitness. For him, a well-tuned body was as least as important as a well-tuned machine.

Fitness was a habit formed early in life. As a teenager, he rebelled against his mother and (first) stepfather and hung out on the street with a group of delinquents, soon learning to give as good as he got. Eventually he was sent to reform school to mend his ways: the Boys Republic, in Chino, California. The young McQueen was number 3188, but, registration numbers aside, the resemblance to any other reform school ends there. There was nothing coercive about the Boys Republic, which functioned more as an apprenticeship center than a house of correction for wayward boys. Indeed, the boys themselves were responsible for administering school discipline. The aim was to encourage responsible behavior and instill confidence through simple teaching methods that taught each boy a trade. High priority was given to sports, using exemplary sporting behavior to inspire team spirit and loyalty. The Boys Republic ethos sought to impart respect for those principles of health and fitness that had been steadily gathering momentum since the early twenty-first century—and in the process, built bonds of confidence among the school's troubled teens.

The notion of caring for the body through physical exercise dates back to antiquity. The ancient Greeks and Romans practiced sports and bodybuilding to emulate the ideal of physical perfection that was embodied in their gods and heroes. Much later, however, in 1884, the French academic Professor Edmond Desbonnet (1867–1953) coined the term "physical culture." "Physical culture," he wrote, "is the art of body-building for its own sake, not to show off. It is also the ABC of sports. I have called my method 'physical culture' to emphasize the difference that distinguishes it from athletics and other forms of gymnastics (whether military or civilian) and physical education . . . . In physical culture, there is no winner and even less a loser. Individuals compete only against themselves, not against one another."

These simple principles, founded on self-discipline and personal effort, were well matched to the gritty, determined character of the young Steve McQueen. He learned how to increase his strength, endurance, and all-round fitness through a daily exercise routine that, for the next few years at least, became a way of life.

McQueen was discharged from Boys Republic in April 1946 at age 16. Whatever else life held in store for him, he had acquired a strong sense of values and a taste for physical training. The next few years brought a rootless existence, wandering from the streets of New York into the arms of the Merchant Marine and the filthy deck of a grimy cargo ship. He set sail without looking back, searching for some far-off El Dorado where the sun was said to take the sting out of poverty. The ship was the SS *Alpha*, a Greek arms carrier that put to sea from Yonkers.

The moment the ship was out of harbor, McQueen was assigned a variety of chores, each one more revolting than the last. The only way he could cope was to work out with weights, iron bars, or whatever makeshift equipment he could lay his hands on. In the wee small hours of the morning, watched by jeering seamen and stevedores, he would run on the rusted decks and perform a grueling series of pushups.

On arrival in the Dominican Republic, McQueen switched to another cargo. This time he was careful to sign on as ship's carpenter, having realized that he needed some trade skill to get back to the United States. Next stop was Port Arthur, Texas, working not as a carpenter, as it happens, but in an up-market brothel. A whole new world of emotions awaited him, along with another form of physical exercise that called for a different kind of stamina. He took to it like a duck to water.

Next came a whole string of jobs—on an oilrig, selling colored pencils in a fairground, lumberjacking in the remotest part of Ontario. At the age of 17, he joined the United States Marine Corps. While military discipline proved quite an ordeal for the young McQueen, he seized the opportunity to indulge his love of mechanical things and trained as a mechanic. He also got back into training, working out on a daily basis as a way of coping with strict drill sergeants and meager food rations that often left him hungry.

In the end, despite countless punishment details and disciplinary sanctions, McQueen distinguished himself with an act of heroism that required exceptional physical prowess. In recognition of his

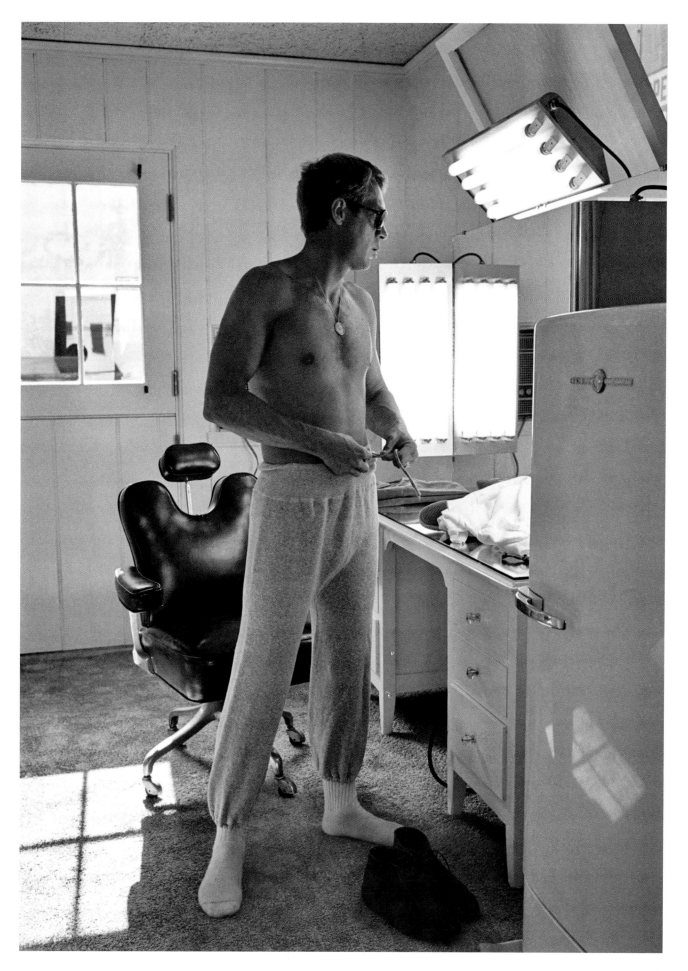

action, he was chosen to join an official escort protecting President Harry Truman's yacht—a signal honor that convinced him more than ever to keep up the exercise habit.

McQueen was one of the very first actors to hone his physique, not only for the sake of his image but also to keep his body fine-tuned for work. His body was a key asset. Frank Sinatra, who McQueen would later work with, also understood the importance of physical fitness and would swim lengths every morning in his pool to build up his lung power.

McQueen showed similar initiative. He was one of the first in his profession to install a home gym, long before the idea of private sports facilities caught on. This personal approach to fitness was the domain of a privileged, wealthy few—Steve McQueen for instance. Following his first real successes, first on television and then the big screen, he moved into a luxurious house on Solar Drive where he had a room outfitted with the very latest in fitness equipment. Sand-filled punch bag, complete set of weights, bodybuilding equipment, treadmill—you name it, McQueen's gym had it. And to guide him through new exercises targeting specific muscles (whether for a role or a race), he engaged the services of a professional fitness coach. It would be another 30 years before personal trainers became commonplace.

In the mid-1960s, McQueen added martial arts to his fitness repertoire—mainly Jeet Kune Do—and went to work on his reflexes and concentration. His master was none other than Bruce Lee, who had recently opened a dojo in Los Angeles. McQueen was one of a select group of highly motivated pupils, and he would remain friends with Bruce until Lee's premature death in 1973. Swimming was another of McQueen's favorite sports. All of his homes featured private pools. If this conjures up images of ornate swimming pools surrounded by bikini-clad starlets in high heels—think again. Kidney-shaped pools may have been popular with Hollywood producers and the retired folk in Malibu, but they never caught on with McQueen. His pools were strictly for exercise.

McQueen's wholehearted commitment to fitness comes across on the big screen. He often played manly heroes: men like Josh Randall, the outlaw bounty hunter in *Wanted: Dead or Alive*; or the fire chief in *The Towering Inferno*; or the big-hearted seaman in *The Sand Pebbles*; and of course Michael Delaney, the virtuoso racer in the film *Le Mans*. He could also manage characters much younger than his own age: McQueen was 36 when he played the 19-year-old lead in *Nevada Smith*. The most symbolic scene in any of his movies has to be the solitary confinement sequence in *Papillon*. McQueen plays a petty criminal sentenced to a penitentiary on Devil's Island, French Guiana, for a crime he did not commit. Recaptured after countless escape attempts, he is thrown into solitary: a damp black hole where he suffers the cruelty of total isolation and darkness for a full two years. He survives, seriously debilitated, but with his dreams of escape and life intact, by exercising in his cell, performing continuous pushups to keep himself in shape.

"When I believe in something, I fight like hell for it." As the future would show time and again, our man was in deadly earnest when he said this to Sanford Meisner, director of Neighborhood Playhouse where McQueen first took up acting in 1952. His commitment to fitness and performance became a life principle, echoing the idea first expressed by French author Jean Giraudoux that "sport is a matter of assigning to the body some of the strongest virtues of the soul." That commitment put him on the road to excellence and the path to glory.

The daily two-hour workout, a routine that McQueen stuck to religiously—sometimes working out at the Paramount fitness center, sometimes in the private gym he had installed at his home.

For McQueen, a perfectly tuned physique was essential for what he loved best: motor racing. Like most extreme sports, racing takes a heavy toll on the body. Some events last several hours, pushing reflexes and concentration to the limit. On hot days, race car cockpit temperatures can easily exceed 120 degrees Fahrenheit.

McQueen took a strict line on fitness. In the early 1960s, he was among the first Hollywood actors to hone his physique for the sake of his image on the silver screen.

ANYONE CAUGHT
IN HERE
BETTER HAVE A
DAMNED GOOD REASON

Pages 86–89:
Steve and first wife, Neile Adams, relaxing at their home in Palm Springs, California.

Following pages: At home in 1963, pretending to drive a
race car for the photographer.

McQUEEN

SPEED AND THE
SILVER SCREEN

McQUEEN
SPEED AND THE SILVER SCREEN

McQUEEN SPEED AND THE SILVER SCREEN

Steve McQueen and speed went hand in hand. However famous for his cool, understated performances, he is mainly remembered for some of the most jaw-dropping high-speed action sequences in cinematic history. Solar Productions, formed by McQueen in 1960, made films dear to the heart of a Hollywood nonconformist who lived for speed. His movies featured motorcars and motorcycles, of course, but also dune buggies, gliders, and all sorts of weird and wonderful machines that McQueen included not just by chance or habit, but because for him they represented a ticket to freedom. Movement and acceleration brought a form of liberation. Reading between the lines, what comes across in all of the characters he played is a multifaceted personality, full of enthusiasm on the one hand but also prone to doubt. His filmography sometimes sheds light on the real-life Steve McQueen and vice versa.

A moviemaker doesn't just pick a car because it happens to suit the decor. The car makes a powerful statement about the character. This is even more the case in the movies than in real life, albeit with the exaggeration and caricature that tends to happen with this kind of symbolism and that cinema inevitably fosters and even accentuates. The choice of vehicle is quite deliberate, calculated to help the viewer build up a picture of the character—personality, tastes, and ambitions—as quickly as possible.

Bearing that in mind, it is telling that Steve McQueen portraying Thomas Crown has a choice of two cars. In town, our billionaire gentlemen thief drives a Rolls-Royce Silver Shadow, one of the most exclusive and luxurious cars around at the time, built to customer order by London coachbuilders H. J. Mulliner and Park Ward. The car is a status symbol on four wheels, synonymous with elegance and success. And it's not your ordinary chauffeur-driven limo, mind you, but a chic coupe Crown himself drives. If this suggests some political freethinker who thumbs his nose at the status quo, think again, because our rich businessman in fact employs a butler, John. Crown simply loves to flaunt his appetite for freedom and the modern lifestyle that goes with it—as he so vividly demonstrates by roaring across the dunes in a brawny Corvair-powered Meyers Manx dune buggy, unbothered by road markings and far from the outward trappings of civilization.

Set against this is the Italian car driven by Crown's opponent/love interest, Vicki Anderson. She owns a Ferrari. Not just any Ferrari, but a Ferrari 275 GTS/4 NART Spyder, one of ten limited-edition

and highly desirable convertibles specially built for Luigi Chinetti and his North American Racing Team (NART). Faye Dunaway never actually drives the car in the film. The Ferrari is purely a symbol of her character's capacity for speed, daring, and reckless living. The car is a symbolic and metaphorical presence: the unmoving presence of the car and Dunaway's character cleverly juxtaposed with the film's fast-moving polo scene.

Dune racing aside, what really lights Thomas Crown's fire is polo, the fastest of all stick-and-ball games. The spectacular "cavalry charge" displays his courage and skill in the heat of the action, showing the stuff of which he is really made.

Two further scenes complete Crown's psychological profile: the game of golf that our implacable businessman plays like a real pro and the dreamy glider sequence, Thomas Crown's languorous escape from the everyday world, floating in a poetic silence punctuated only by Michel Legrand's mesmeric melody.

This hymn to peaceful self-elevation makes the high-speed action of the polo game even more effective. For Thomas Crown, like Steve McQueen, equilibrium is achieved only by mixing brief moments of tranquility with frequent, frenetic races against time. The big screen can represent man's battle with himself, or against the society that holds him in check, as a symbolic and highly stylized combat.

The year 1968 saw McQueen make two of his most career-defining movies: first *The Thomas Crown Affair* and then *Bullitt*. Forty years on, both have stood the test of time. And both are key pieces in the complex puzzle of McQueen's personality, riddled with anxiety and conflicting desires.

Just like billionaire robber Thomas Crown, Lieutenant Frank Bullitt of the San Francisco Police Department is a character at odds with his milieu and his own identity. As the product of a troubled childhood marked by frequent brushes with the law, McQueen hesitated before taking on the role of a policeman. But just two days spent with the San Francisco police force changed his mind. When the film was released, he congratulated the police for doing such a good job, adding that the film was his way of paying homage—and something intended to be experienced, not analyzed. Fortunately, the critics thought otherwise, particularly French film critic Max Tessier, who wrote of the actor's coming of age in *Cinéma*

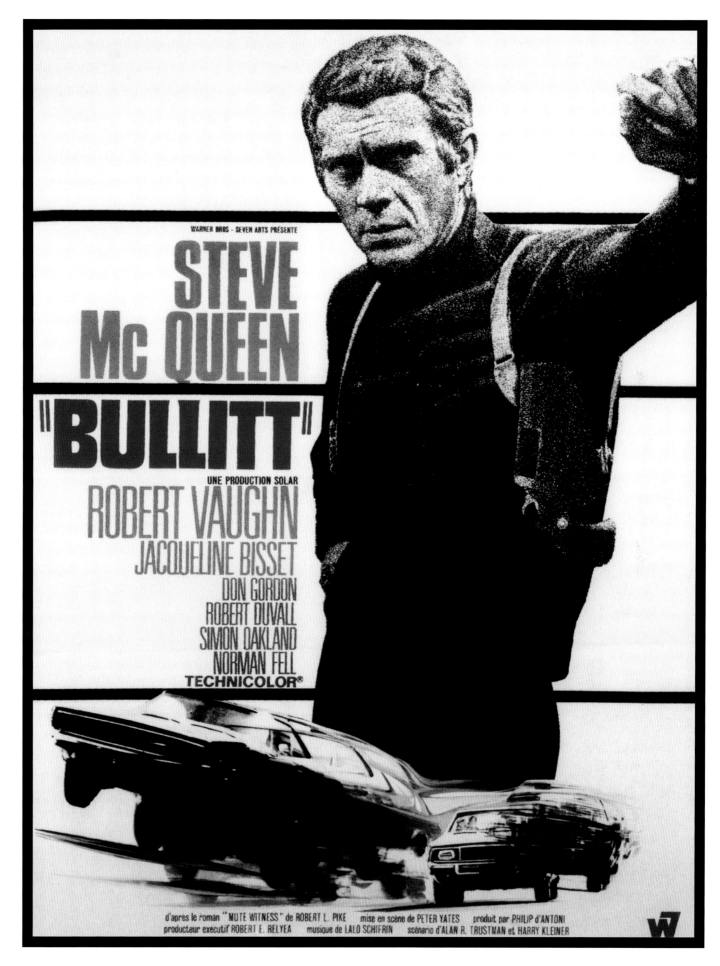

magazine: "*Bullitt* isn't just wallpapering; it isn't just the 'car chase' or 'the airport sequence' . . . . *Bullitt* scratches beneath the surface, exploring every crack in the wall itself thanks to a more seasoned performance by Steve McQueen who achieves better control of his body movements and facial expressions." *Bullitt*, like *The Thomas Crown Affair*, was McQueen's first chance at an extended action sequence (the now classic car chase) that showed the view from the driver's perspective—guaranteed to put you on the edge of your seat. The film *Le Mans* would take that approach one step further.

Interestingly, there are no car chases in *Mute Witness*, the 1966 novel by Robert L. Pike that served as the basis for director Peter Yates' *Bullitt*. McQueen, as co-producer with Warner Bros., nevertheless insisted on an "automotive action scene" from the very earliest versions of the script. But it had to be the real thing, to flesh out his character and give more substance to the movie as a whole. The car chase, like the airport sequence, would become one of the high points in the fight between a maverick detective and an icy politician superbly played by Robert Vaughn. McQueen supervised the preparations and the montage. The 10-minute Oscar-winning chase sequence seems uncut from start to finish. Ford Mustang and Dodge Charger go full throttle through the streets of San Francisco in a high-speed battle between the detective and the gunman, between truth and lies, good and evil. The speed and action are real, complete with overworked suspension, laboring shock absorbers, and tires distorting on high-speed corners. Nothing visual is doctored for effect. The cameras capture every move with breathtaking precision, amplifying the dramatic effect.

The extended car chase through the steep and hilly streets of San Francisco always did promise to be a thrill, and it was. The action takes place in broad daylight, set in San Francisco itself, between Army Street and Guadalupe Canyon Parkway. It took all of McQueen's powers of persuasion (plus a hefty check) and some painstaking groundwork to extract the necessary permissions from an increasingly worried city hall. As for the cars, the "bad guys" drive a 1968 Dodge Charger R/T powered by 375-horsepower, 440-cubic-inch Magnum V-8 topped with a four-barrel carb—a car powerful enough to stay ahead, but too plain-looking to put our hero's Mustang in the shade. The man at the wheel is McQueen's friend, stuntman Bill Hickman; police detective Frank Bullitt drives the Mustang.

The sleek, racy Mustang was the brainchild of Ford's Lee Iacocca and offered a mixture of all-American values with European styling. Launched at the New York World's Fair on April 17, 1964, the Mustang was an immediate success, completely eclipsing its nearest American rival, the Plymouth Barracuda, thanks to its choice of engine options, from the six-cylinder 170 Thriftpower Six to the 289-cubic-inch V-8, plus accessories and chrome details

galore. The Italian coupes and English roadsters of the day suddenly looked decidedly old hat. The 1968 GT 390 Mustang featured in the film was a no-frills American performance car that perfectly suited the taciturn, dogged character of police detective Lieutenant Frank Bullitt.

McQueen asked Ford for two matching fastback coupes—a car with a particularly dynamic profile thanks to its long, sloping roofline. The cars in the film were painted Highland Green Metallic and fitted with 15-inch American Racing Torq-Thrust D alloy wheels. Other features not found on production models include the leather-clad steering wheel. McQueen had the stock steering wheel replaced with a more tasteful three-spoke 1967 Mustang Shelby piece, wrapped in leather by famed upholsterer and drag racer Tony Nancy.

McQueen also had the car stripped of all badges, nameplates, and insignia, furious with Ford for insisting on payment in cash for the cars—a bad call by Ford that made them miss out on a valuable promotion opportunity. In the end, it made little difference. The company is still trading off the success of *Bullitt* decades later, even integrating McQueen in a commercial to promote the launch of the 2005 Mustang .

Of course, *The Thomas Crown Affair* and *Bullitt* weren't the only films featuring McQueen performing stunts with his favorite machines. But they probably rank as the most significant examples of the liberating—one could almost say "salutary"—influence that speed exerted on Steve McQueen. He would pay tribute to this influence again in *Le Mans* and *On Any Sunday*, the latter an iconic 91-minute documentary about motorcyclists and motorcycle racing. Bruce Brown directed the film, and McQueen, who makes occasional appearances, financed it. *On Any Sunday* is an ode to the world of off-road motorcycling and a vibrant homage to the knights of road racing, plus McQueen's all-consuming love of speed. His words of endorsement in the movie trailer: "I think Bruce Brown's motorcycle film *On Any Sunday* is the best thing that has ever happened to motorcycling. The audience is taken on a visual ride in what I believe is finally the definitive film on motorcycling. To me it is an unforgettable film, and I was very happy to be a part of it in some small way."

As usual, McQueen wanted the whole thing to seem as informal and casual as possible. As a devotee of motor sports, in love with off-road racing and crazy about speed, his enthusiasm was genuine—no trace of bravado, just a heartfelt desire to communicate his emotions and convey the thrills and spills of the sport but also the danger, fear, suspense, fierce competition, and agonizing anticipation. He plays himself on screen, on his dirt bike. This isn't McQueen the stuntman-actor extraordinaire of *The Great Escape* (his first big box-office hit). This is McQueen the amateur off-road racer. A humble, more focused McQueen, on familiar ground, surrounded by familiar faces (men like Mert Lawwill and Malcolm Smith), out to compete on equal terms with the most experienced racers. Whatever McQueen's aversion to authority, he always had great respect for the sporting spirit. In the film, he is just an anonymous contestant, caught on camera in various events, including motocross, road racing, beach riding, and desert endurance racing. Born to ride, McQueen wanted to debunk the myth of the outlaw biker, a stereotype often attached to motorcyclists in that period and first perpetrated on screen by a leather-clad Marlon Brando in *The Wild One*. McQueen had reached the age of maturity. At 41, he had seen enough to know that he had not seen it all and know where exactly he was coming from. Racing burned inside McQueen like a fever. "Racing is life," he once said. "Anything before or after is just waiting." *On Any Sunday* touched a lot of hearts by portraying speed not as something brutal but as the natural corollary of a certain milieu and way of life. The film was a huge success when it was released—some consolation, no doubt, for the resounding failure of *Le Mans*.

Setting that aside, it is certain that McQueen will be remembered as one of the finest exponents of speed ever to grace the big screen. Living out our fantasies, embodying our dreams, living the life—this was just a small part of what he achieved, but one that probably carried the most meaning in terms of his life and personality.

Above: McQueen and San Francisco police working on details for the car-chase sequence in *Bullitt*. Shot on location in 1967, the chase required the permission of the city of San Francisco, which was paid handsomely to allow filming downtown between Army Street and Guadalupe Canyon Parkway.

Right: Lieutenant Frank Bullitt drives a Ford Mustang Fastback GT 390—a high-performance version of Ford's famed pony car.

McQueen as San Francisco Police Lieutenant Frank Bullitt. Director Peter Yates' classic won an
Oscar in 1969 for Best Film Editing.

1:06 AM

WHAT WENT INTO THESE FEW SECONDS...

1:07 AM

THE HELL...THE HEROISM...THE HIGH ADVENTURE...

1:08 AM

MAKE FOR THE SCREEN'S GREAT ENTERTAINMENT!

1:09 AM

THE MIRISCH COMPANY PRESENTS JOHN STURGES'

THE GREAT ESCAPE

STEVE McQUEEN   JAMES GARNER   RICHARD ATTENBOROUGH

CO-STARRING JAMES DONALD CHARLES BRONSON DONALD PLEASENCE JAMES COBURN

PRODUCED & DIRECTED BY JOHN STURGES SCREENPLAY BY JAMES CLAVELL & W.R. BURNETT BASED UPON THE BOOK BY PAUL BRICKHILL MUSIC ELMER BERNSTEIN COLOR BY DE LUXE PANAVISION A MIRISCH-ALPHA PICTURE RELEASED THRU UNITED ARTISTS

Above and right: McQueen stand-in Bud Ekins jumps a barbed-wire fence in 1963's *The Great Escape*. Had McQueen had his way, he would have done all the motorcycle stunts himself. His insurers thought otherwise, much to the relief of director John Sturges and the film's producers.

The Great Escape was directed by John Sturges (far right) and starred Steve McQueen, James Coburn (in the side car), James Garner (riding pillion behind McQueen), Richard Attenborough, and Charles Bronson.

WL-66320

McQueen's studio contract forbade him from racing when filming, mainly for insurance reasons. But the moment he heard those three magic words—"That's a wrap"—it was straight back to the track.

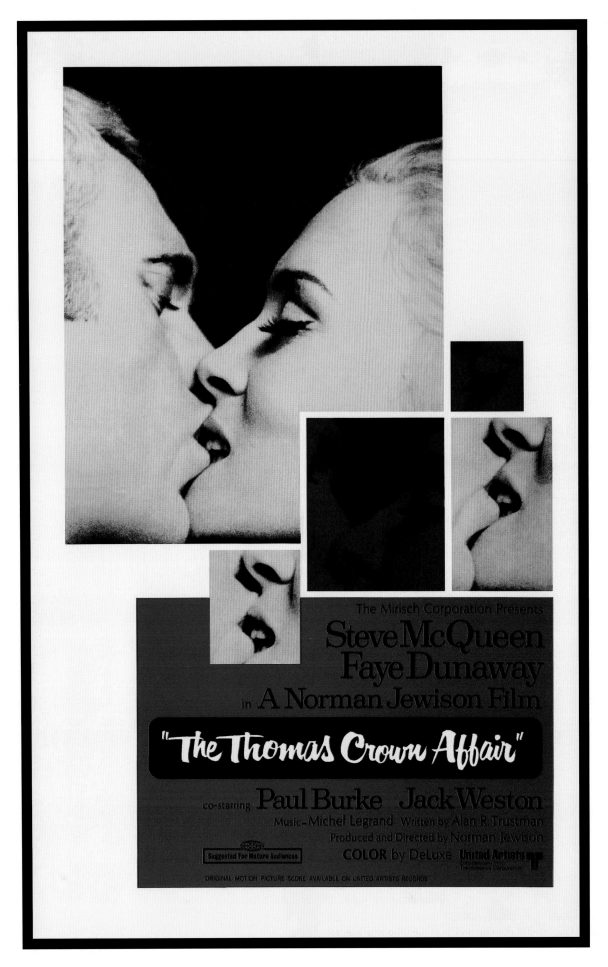

A movie poster for *The Thomas Crown Affair* (1968), featuring Faye Dunaway and Steve McQueen, lip-locked. Michel Legrand's inimitable musical touch won the film an Oscar the following year for best original score.

Above and right: The famous beach ride in *The Thomas Crown Affair*, which McQueen had to fight to have included in the script. Crown guns his Corvair-engined dune buggy across the beach, devouring the dunes with the delicious Faye Dunaway at his side. Her career had just taken off following her award-winning performance the previous year in *Bonnie and Clyde*.

Steve McQueen, aged 38, as thrill-seeking billionaire Thomas Crown, in a role that nicely combined his love of speed with his love of acting. Skillfully directed by Norman Jewison, the film is packed with adrenaline-fueled activities. Motor-racing, gliding, polo playing—McQueen couldn't have asked for more.

Above and right: Thomas Crown drives a Rolls-Royce Silver Shadow, one of the most exclusive and luxurious cars of its time, built to custom-order by London coachbuilders H. J. Mulliner and Park Ward. The car was McQueen's choice, calculated to make his character even more plausible as a gentleman thief.

McQUEEN
RACING IS LIFE

McQUEEN
RACING IS LIFE

McQUEEN RACING IS LIFE

In the mid-1960s, McQueen decided to combine his love of racing with his love of acting by making a movie dedicated to the world of motorsports. His idea was to put the audience in the driver's seat of a racing car at speeds of 225 miles per hour on the Mulsanne Straight. At speeds like that, he said, you were off in another dimension, another world.

The subject matter, however, was far from obvious. Anyone could film racing drivers whizzing down a track, but this by itself hardly constituted the makings of a good story. In 1965, McQueen teamed up once again with John Sturges, director of *The Great Escape*. The plan was to make a film about the angst of motor-racing called *Day of the Champion*, but production was shelved while McQueen was away in Taiwan finishing the filming of *The Sand Pebbles*.

In his absence, director John Frankenheimer beat him to it with *Grand Prix*, a film about four Formula 1 drivers competing for the world championship. Starring McQueen's friend and associate James Garner and co-starring Yves Montand and Eva Marie-Saint, the film was an international success and won three Oscars on its release in 1966. Hollywood figured that another film on the same theme would be dangerously repetitive, and *Day of the Champion* was put on indefinite hold.

But McQueen hadn't abandoned the idea—far from it. He kept turning it over in his mind, aiming for a film that would be his personal statement about speed and motorsports. His ambition was to show something that had never been shown before. More than that, he wanted to capture the exact experience of competition racing in all its dimensions—mechanical, sensual, human, and psychological. His enthusiasm for the project comes across loud and clear in this 1969 interview with *Motor Trend* magazine: "I'm thrilled because we think we'll be able to do things with the camera no one has ever done before. For instance, we'd like to effectively capture the speed of 220–225mph at Mulsanne. If we can, cinematically, give people a pleasant feeling and yet give them the sheer sense of speed at the edge of infinity, then we've created greatness."

The race he had in mind was the grueling 24 Hours of Le Mans, described by McQueen as "the greatest endurance race in the world." And he should know. As a seasoned endurance driver, McQueen already had several events under his belt and was particularly noted for his performance in the 12 Hours of Sebring.

He knew that endurance racing was not just about competing with other drivers, other cars, or other constructors. It was also about competing against himself and against time, pushing his body to the limit as he drove the asphalt in an enclosed steel cage, and being more cunning than the other guy in a battle against the elements, fatigue, night, noise, and heat.

The rigors of endurance racing have to be experienced to be understood. When the cockpit of an enclosed race car is stripped of all unnecessary weight, the temperature by day can climb to more than 120 degrees Fahrenheit. The noise of the engine within that confined space is deafening. The driver is squeezed into a racing suit complete with gloves, balaclava, helmet, and boots and strapped in tight. At speeds pushing 150 miles per hour (average for Le Mans), the body is forced back into the seat, the legs feel like lead, unable to stretch, and the feet get horribly cramped from the constant action on the bare metal pedals. The eyes sting and burn as they flick incessantly from track to dashboard, tachometer, warning lights, and rearview mirror. But the battle—however punishing—is more than worth it for the sensation of liberation and fulfillment.

Equally grueling is the race against time, which motor racing distorts in strange ways. Speed compresses space. Minutes can seem shorter. Seconds can seem longer. For the person behind the wheel, the tension at the start is unbearable. The clock seems to take forever. The heart and temples race faster as the moments tick away. And they're off! Engines roaring full throttle, exhausts blatting, and pistons thundering. The first lap is a cavalry charge. Then the cars begin their endless circling, spinning in orbit around that strange Saturn that we call a racetrack.

Now comes the first change of driver, fresh hands on the wheel. And you wait. Wait until it's your turn again. Wait in the paddock with the mechanics or in a small trailer. Drink to quench your thirst; eat to restore your energy levels; try to catch some sleep. But never really managing to relax. Itching to get back into the fray and cross swords with the other drivers. With that eternal gnawing sensation in the pit of your stomach. Drunk on speed. Scared by danger. Aware of the ever-present risks—the accident lurking around every bend. Any lap might end in disaster or glory. Hours with nothing to do except do like the spectators and watch the cars circling in a balletic rotation that is seemingly without end. All people remember, from start to finish, are the feats of daring. Not the waiting and frustration, suspense, and exhilaration that happens in between.

It is unfair to dismiss *Le Mans* as nothing more than an ode to speed. McQueen set out to portray the passion of racing as accurately as possible. There was never any question of building cheap movie

sets. What he needed was a full-length feature film, shot entirely on location.

The 24 Hours of Le Mans was born in the Sarthe region of France and first contested in 1923. McQueen's original intention was to compete in the race himself, much encouraged by his very honorable second place at Sebring at the wheel of a Porsche 908. He had professional racer Jackie Stewart in mind as co-driver. Solar Productions (McQueen's movie production company) bought a new Porsche 917 from the Porsche factory. This was one of the coolest, most ferocious machines of its time: aerodynamic fiberglass body, aluminum chassis, and the driver's seat so far forward that the driver's feet reached beyond the front-wheel axle. The car was powered by a mid-mounted, air-cooled, flat-12 engine of 4.5-liters, developing 580 horsepower. Weight was 1,760 pounds (under 800 kg), giving the 917 an enviable power-to-weight ratio.

But in the end the studio refused to play ball, deciding that putting its star in the race was an insurance risk that was too great. After weeks of negotiations, Cinema Center Films vetoed the idea, but struck a compromise. McQueen himself could not compete in the race, but his Porsche 908 could, cunningly kitted out as a camera car. For the sake of absolute realism, all the scenes featuring McQueen at the wheel would be driven post-race by our man himself, driving the Porsche 917 at speeds approaching 225 miles per hour (360 kilometers per hour). Clever film editing would take care of the rest.

As both star and producer of *Le Mans*, McQueen was taking a big gamble, but figured his film was more than worth it. In spring 1970, the entire film crew shipped out to La Sarthe. Their first task was to film the race—a big challenge in itself. The winner of the previous year's event was Ford. But with the Ford GT40 clearly on the way out, mainly due to lack of factory backing, its ingenious designer, John Wyer, switched to the Porsche 917. The 1970 Le Mans event shaped up to be a battle between the Porsche 917s and their sworn rivals, the Ferrari 512s.

Scuderia Ferrari entered four cars. These, plus seven privateer Ferraris made up the Maranello grid. The Ferrari 512 boasted an ultra-lightweight aluminum structure and a 5-liter V-12 engine pumping out nearly 575 horsepower. It was a worthy opponent for the Porsche 917.

The Porsche factory pinned its hopes on John Wyer, the man who steered Aston Martin to victory in 1959, then Ford for two years in a row in 1968 and 1969. He now ran the Porsche works team. It was also John Wyer who brought blue and orange to motor racing. Back when the GT40 was still in the development stage, Wyer became friends with a young businessman who counted himself as a gentlemen-driver—a certain Grady Davis, Gulf Oil vice president.

Gulf Oil sponsored Wyer to improve its corporate image—what every oil company wanted at that time. Davis and Wyer dared to do what no one had ever before dared to do: not just scatter the bodywork with stickers, but paint the entire car in the sponsor's colors. This was back when race cars wore national colors, British Racing Green, Rosso Corsa (Italian racing red), or Bleu de France (French racing blue). The color Davis and Wyer chose was not the darker corporate Gulf blue, but the now famous powder blue of the much smaller Gulf-owned Wiltshire Oil Company. Davis's personal GT40 caused a sensation when it ran in blue and orange livery at the 1967 24 Hours of Daytona. Piloted by Jacky Ickx, the car finished first in class. Blue and orange were off to a good start.

In the film, McQueen plays Porsche driver Michael Delaney, running in Gulf-Wyer livery and numbered 20. Jo Siffert and Brian Redman actually drove the car in the race. To avoid continuity errors, McQueen wore Jo Siffert's suit for all the post-race filming—white with blue and orange stripes and the Gulf insignia. He even wore the same watch—a nice touch, never mind that there were strictly commercial reasons for doing so. (Swiss driver Siffert was Swiss watchmaker TAG Heuer's first official brand ambassador.)

"Product placement" didn't officially exist in cinema back then, but property masters certainly looked for opportunities just as they do today, leaning on key members of the production team (set designers, decorators, dressers, etc.) to ensure that certain brands—tobacco, alcohol, and other props used by the actors— were featured in a movie.

When now-honorary TAG Heuer chairman Jack Heuer learned that shooting was about to start at La Sarthe, he moved swiftly into action. Time being of the essence—no pun intended—he sent an envoy to La Sarthe bearing gifts in the form of the revolutionary Heuer Monaco, a large, square-cased, black-faced chronograph that in the event proved just too far advanced for its market (production was discontinued in 1975). It cost a heavy customs fine to get the gift to La Sarthe, but no matter. The star of *Le Mans* was wearing the Monaco on Day One of shooting.

A few days later, McQueen noticed that he wasn't the only one to get a wristwatch from Heuer—so too had several of the technicians and heads of production. Furious at having fallen for such a cheap sales trick, he tore the watch off and smashed it to the ground. Producer Lee H. Katzin had to intervene, pointing out that there was no question of changing props now that filming was underway and doing his best to calm the actor down. McQueen relented and agreed to wear the watch until the very last take—but not one day longer.

Jack Heuer had no intention of tricking McQueen and requested a meeting to set the record straight. He had invoices drawn up to prove that the other watches had in fact been bought by the crew, copycat style. McQueen invited Heuer to lunch on set and sent his private plane to Paris to collect him. But the lunch never happened because, in typically unpredictable fashion, McQueen took off into the Sarthe countryside on his motorcycle. Heuer stepped down from the small twin-engine aircraft to discover that McQueen's reputation for spontaneity was fully justified. McQueen's loss, Heuer's gain: our Swiss watchmaker had a tête-à-tête lunch with Elga Andersen, the female interest in the film, and eventually got McQueen's permission to use some of the images from the film for corporate purposes.

Steve McQueen's version of the 1970 Le Mans gives a fictional victory to John Wyer, whose drivers did indeed put up a terrific fight. But in reality, while Porsches took all three places on the podium (multiple accidents knocked out all but two of the Ferraris) a Gulf-Wyer Porsche was not one of them. The winner was the Porsche Salzburg 917. The Gulf-Wyer 917 raced to victory only in the film.

For car historians, the 1970 event is particularly memorable as the first race that broke with the traditional Le Mans–style start. This running start had been Le Mans tradition dating back to the race's earliest days. The cars lined up diagonally on one side of the pit lane, in order of qualifying, with drivers on the other side. At the signal, drivers were required to sprint across to their cars, jump in, start them, and go. But by 1969, the Le Mans–style start was considered outdated and dangerous. That year, young Belgian driver Jacky Ickx walked to his car while others ran, protesting that cars took off so quickly and in such chaos that accidents were inevitable. To save time, drivers didn't always bother to strap themselves in securely or check that their doors were shut properly. Ickx's demonstration did the trick, and the Le Mans–style start was discarded for the 1970 race. The film shows drivers strapped in and ready to go, finger poised over the starter button as the tension mounts.

Le Mans was a commercial flop for McQueen. With hindsight, it's hard to see how it could have been otherwise, given the weak, unconnected storyline and its overreliance on sometimes unremarkable racing action. From a strictly cinematographic point of view, the film is barely watchable—a treat for real racing enthusiasts perhaps, but much too noisy, long, and uneven for an "ordinary" moviegoer. But this very failure offers resounding proof that McQueen did what he set out to do. The film definitely stands as one of the most stunning cinematic accounts of motor racing and the magic of competition and speed.

Opposite and above: Between shoots on the set of *Le Mans*, McQueen gets to sit in a Brabham F2 and gains some tips from its test driver, British Formula 1 pilot Derek Bell.

Steve McQueen takes you for a drive in the country. The country is France. The drive is at 200 MPH!

STEVE McQUEEN

A CINEMA CENTER FILMS PRESENTATION

Written by HARRY KLEINER · Music by MICHEL LEGRAND · Executive Producer ROBERT E. RELYEA · Produced by JACK N. REDDISH
Directed by LEE H. KATZIN · A SOLAR PRODUCTION · PANAVISION® Color by DE LUXE · A NATIONAL GENERAL PICTURES RELEASE

Lee H. Katzin's *Le Mans* was released in 1971. For co-producer Steve McQueen, the film marked the fulfillment of a long-held dream to celebrate his love of speed and motor-racing on screen. A generous budget allowed him to feature some 25 outstanding machines, including four Porsche 917s, one Porsche 908/2, three Lola T70 Mk III GT coupes, four Ferrari 512Ss, and one Ford GT40.

Above and right: McQueen's character in the film *Le Mans* drives a Porsche 917K (pictured right).
One of the most formidable machines of its time, the 917 combined clean, aerodynamic lines and
a fiberglass body with a ferocious 4.5-liter 12-cylinder engine developing 580 horsepower. Weight
was just 1,760 pounds, which gave the car an enviable power-to-weight ratio.

The average speed of cars competing in the 1971 Le Mans was 156 miles per hour. The director used a variety of onboard cameras to convey the sense of speed, including one mounted on McQueen's helmet (left) and another on the hood of a Ford GT40 (above).

Le Mans was essentially a film for racing buffs and, as such, doomed to fail at the box-office. But it definitely stands as one of the most stunning cinematic accounts of motor-racing ever produced, complete with all the noise, pace, and knife-edge tension.

McQueen's 917 trails a Ferrari 512S.

McQUEEN'S
GARAGE

McQUEEN'S GARAGE

McQUEEN'S GARAGE

Passionate people tend to act on impulse, and McQueen was no exception in this respect. Many of his toys were love at first sight. As a discerning connoisseur, seasoned mechanic and experienced racer, McQueen had an insatiable appetite for propulsion, thrills, and speed. Machines fed that craving. Each one had to be more beautiful, powerful, and higher-performing than the last. Machines were meshed with the fabric of McQueen's everyday life, on-screen and even more so in reality. They are part of the story that describes a man who was hard-wired for freedom, and the thrill that comes from extremes.

McQueen wasn't really a collector from a curatorial perspective. Collecting implies thoughtfulness—a focus that ultimately gives cohesion to the collection, whether or not this was the intention at the outset. McQueen owned about 100 classic motorcycles, along with assorted machines on two wheels and four and sometimes with wings. But these were mainly bought to satisfy his wants and needs: a dirt-bike so he could compete in off-road races; a sports car so he could compete on the track; an airplane so he could soar weightless in the sky, freed from the illness that was eating him alive.

These days, it is the turn of other people to collect McQueen's machines, partly for the pleasure of collecting but also for the added fascination of celebrity memorabilia. Some might call it superstitious fetishism, but there is something strangely satisfying about owning objects once owned by a cult figure like McQueen. Big auction houses like Bonhams do their best to nurture that interest. McQueen's bikes, cars, airplanes, childhood toys, and personal effects regularly come up for auction, fetching ever higher prices that have long since ceased to reflect the intrinsic value of the object itself. When you look at each one in turn, they all fit together like the pieces of a jigsaw puzzle. McQueen's Indian motorcycle, his Persol shades with blue lenses and collapsible frame, his iconic biker jacket . . . these are not just what he wore or what he drove. They are key elements in a lifestyle that was the envy of his fans. Though to him, they were everyday objects that he took for granted.

One thing is for certain: in terms of style, Steve McQueen never put a foot wrong. From the start, he had an unerring instinct for what is seen to this day as the last word in elegance and chic. Style came naturally to him. He went from New York to Sunset Boulevard without passing "go," stopping to window-shop along the way at Ernie McAfee Engineering, the Italian sports-car dealership that specialized in cars with evocative names like Ferrari, Moretti, and OSCA.

After his first wife Neile Adams crashed the couple's newly acquired Corvette, McQueen lost no time in replacing it with another toy. Not another American car but a much cuter, tastier European number— something not unlike the MG TC he owned in New York, or the racy Austin-Healey 100M he had when he got married. What he chose was a rare Italian roadster, purchased from Ernie McAfee for $4,995 (pretty much all the money McQueen had at the time). The car was a metallic gray Siata 208S Spider.

Siata (Societa Italiana Auto Trasformazioni Accessori) started as a tuning accessories shop in Turin, founded in 1926 by Giorgio Ambrosini. It became famous as a supplier of performance parts to Fiat and after World War II turned to making and selling sports cars and touring sedans under its own name. Siata's first proprietary car was the Siata Amica (1949), a pretty little cabriolet modeled on the Fiat 500 Topolino.

In 1952, the now established Siata used the famed, Fiat-built 1,996cc Otto Vu engine as the basis for a new creation: a racy, open two-seater, powered by eight cylinders in a V configuration (Otto Vu is Italian for "V-8"). This was the 208S Spider. Just 35 examples would be built, and McQueen's was chassis number BS 523, registration number MTY 9065. The Siata featured taut, elegant, somewhat aggressive styling, penned by Giovanni Michelotti and built by Bertone: wide front radiator grille and headlights set flush with the wing. Quite like the AC Bristol, and not a little reminiscent of what Ferrari was doing at the time. McQueen, in fact, removed the front nose badge and replaced it with the Maranello prancing-horse shield, dubbing the car his "little Ferrari."

Within a year, the Siata was back for sale at Ernie McAfee Engineering. McQueen had reluctantly agreed to part with it, under constant pressure from the studio to rein in his speed-freak habits. The car sold for $4,500 to Dr. Bruce Sand, an intern at UCLA Medical School. Sold, but sorely missed by its former owner as the young doctor found out the following summer when a rising Hollywood star took him for the race car drive of his life . . . . As related by Matt Stone in *McQueen's Machines*, "This guy in a Ford convertible comes up alongside and motioned for us to pull over," recalled Sand. "It was McQueen. We pulled over, and he said, 'I want to drive.' So my friend got out, and I got into the Siata's passenger seat. McQueen hopped in and took me for one exciting ride." Foot down, flat-out on the deserted roads, McQueen tore up Coldwater Canyon before hanging a U-turn at Mulholland. Bruce Sand held on tight but could sense he was in good hands. McQueen never uttered a word. Back

on Sunset, he pulled up alongside his Ford, got in, and left. The fun and games were over.

Next up, the Porsche 356 Speedster 1600 Super, McQueen's first brand-new car. Black paintwork, black folding top, and fitted with Rudge knock-off wheels like a race car. Zippy little 1950s sports cars didn't get any zippier than that. The Porsche Speedster was every sports-car buff's dream. And unlike the impossibly expensive Ferraris, Maseratis and Aston Martins, this one was almost affordable.

The Porsche 356 was a blueprint for sports-car success. It was the brainchild of Ferry Porsche, based on the VW Beetle designed by his father, Ferdinand Porsche, Sr. From 1950 to 1955, a sequence of ever higher performing engines confirmed the growing reputation of the young German brand in sports-car racing. The Porsche 356 coupe with its elegantly curved windshield and synchro gearbox was sports car driving at its most glamorous. Too much so, indeed, for Porsche's then U.S. importer Max Hoffman who persuaded Ferry Porsche to make a simpler, cheaper roadster version specifically for the West Coast, where the weather is good year-round. And so the Speedster was born. Launched in 1954, it was a hit from the start.

This was one road-hugging German speed machine, stripped down to look like a race car. It had a cut-down windshield, the cockpit was purged of everything but bare essentials, and it was finished to strict Stuttgart standards. No wind-down windows; unlined folding top; extra-large white Bakelite steering wheel; dashboard grab handle on the passenger—correction—"co-driver" side. Hoffman wasn't looking to increase his profit margins, but to improve brand visibility with a car that turned heads. And the Speedster certainly did that. It topped the charts right to the end of production in 1959—a favorite with bright young things and blue-eyed Hollywood stars like James Dean.

Hoffman took great pride in the car he delivered to McQueen in 1958. It was a brand-new roadster, in black with matching top and interior—very tasty indeed. "Less was more" for McQueen when it came to style, so he had some of the chrome-plated accessories removed along with the Reutter coachbuilder badge. The car was ultra-cool and also powerful: McQueen had opted for the Speedster 1600 Super, which delivered a good 15 horsepower more than the "normal" version (75 horsepower compared with 60 horsepower).

McQueen and his Speedster devoured the miles and also went racing together—our man's cue to explore new pastures. In 1959, he sold the Porsche and treated himself to a real race car: the fabulous Colin Chapman—designed Lotus Eleven. This was the machine that took him from driver to racing driver, light and with all the punch required to keep him happy. But McQueen always missed his little Speedster. Years later, he would buy it back, just as he bought back his fabulous and very exclusive 1957 Jaguar XK-SS.

Some Porsches are inseparable from the memory of Steve McQueen. The 356 Speedster is one of them. Another is the slate gray 911S that he drove in the role of racing driver Michael Delaney, at the start of the film Le Mans. And not forgetting, of course, the 908 and 917 that he drove in other races. But for most collectors and racing buffs, the most fantastic machine McQueen ever owned was his 1957 Jaguar XK-SS. It was also his own personal favorite, the car he cherished until the day he died. The Jaguar XK-SS really did have everything—particularly for McQueen who showed a proper appreciation of the qualities it owed to Jaguar's racing pedigree.

Jaguar dominated top-level motor sport in the 1950s, overtaking its competitors with the C-Type then the D, which was three times a winner at Le Mans. Off the back of this success, the Coventry firm's founder William Lyons saw a chance to issue the D-Type in a form to suit rich gentlemen racers. But sadly, only 67 examples were constructed.

True, the car was not road-legal, which limited its use and went against British habits of the time—amateur racers liked to drive to events to save money. As a result the D-Type was a commercial failure. At the end of the 1956 season, Jaguar found itself with 25 cars left unsold. Both British race car driver Duncan Hamilton and American coachbuilder Bob Blake had each modified a D-Type to road spec. Whether Jaguar followed the lead of either man is open to debate, but in any case on January 21, 1957, the company announced production of the XK Super Sport. The XK-SS project was underway.

The goal was a machine very close to the fabulous D-Type, winner of Le Mans—and it took Jaguar engineers just three days to convert a naked D-Type chassis into a rolling XK-SS prototype. The sleek profile of aerodynamicist Malcolm Sayer's original D-Type would sport a little baggage carrier on the rear deck, thin chrome bumpers, small windshield with wipers, fixed side windows, and a small top to complete the road details. A passenger seat was added to create a two-seat cockpit—spartan, but still reasonably comfortable and well protected from drafts. A swinging passenger door was cut into the aluminum coachwork.

The finished product weighed little more than 2,000 pounds (992 kilos). Throbbing at the heart of this plane-without-wings was a real monster of an engine: a 3.4 liter, dual overhead camshaft (DOHC) in-line six-cylinder, served by triple 45mm DCOE Webers. Quite simply the best and most brutally powerful package around at the time. The DOHC engine came with a four-speed all-synchromesh manual gearbox, and developed 250 horsepower at 5,750 rpm. Four-wheel disc brakes gave excellent stopping power—though stopping was not what the Jaguar was about. Acceleration was the thing: 0 to 60 in just 4.7 seconds, with a top speed of 180 miles-per-hour-plus.

It was performance unheard of back then, especially for a "road" car. The Jaguar was every inch an explosive cocktail of power and sports handling, with a supple, feline feel that made it a dream to drive.

In the midst of converting the Ds to XK-SSs, something quite unexpected happened in the works. On February 12, 1957, just 22 days after the car's official launch, fire gutted the Browns Lane Jaguar factory, destroying most of the tooling, the spare parts inventory and nine almost completed cars. Production of Jaguar cars was brought to a halt. It started up again two or three days later, but that was the end of the XK-SS project. Only 16 were completed. Back in 1957, they were priced at around 6,900 Pounds Sterling. Today, an XK-SS fetches six or seven figures. The fact that Steve McQueen was among the lucky owners obviously helps.

The Jag's first owner was public works contractor James Peterson in April 1957. A keen sports-car buff, Peterson helped to build the Riverside International Raceway where McQueen distinguished himself on several occasions. Back then, the XK-SS, chassis Type D 569, was white with red interior.

Peterson kept the car for eight months then sold it to 1950s radio broadcaster Bill Leyden. McQueen would stop to look at the Jag whenever he spotted it in the Hollywood Studios parking lot, or driving past on Sunset Boulevard. When he heard that Leyden was looking for a buyer, in 1958, his heart missed a beat. Having first sold his crazy idea to first wife Neile Adams, McQueen shelled out $5,000 and the car was his—or rather hers, since it was Neile's signature on the check. McQueen then took the car for prepping by Hollywood car customizer Tony Nancy, who repainted the exterior British Racing Green and reupholstered the interior in black leather. The chrome luggage rack was remounted on the rear deck and a small glove compartment was built into the dash by McQueen's friend and painter/customizer Von Dutch. The car registration number was JNH 809, and its new owner nicknamed it the *Green Rat*. So much for the preparations—time to hit the road.

The Jaguar was everything that McQueen wanted from a car, hence its emblematic status among the many cars that he owned. Powerful, classy, modern, and understated, the XK-SS was an uncompromising performer. Ignition on, one light touch of the starter, and that in-line six with its triple carbs was ready to go. The engine note was a throaty, almost animal growl. But there was nothing savage about the Coventry Jaguar. For all its competition pedigree, it could be as docile as a lamb. The driver's seat held the body in a natural upright position, arms relaxed on armrests, with a good view of the road and the shapely contours of the hood. The pedals were spaced wide enough for street shoes, but close enough for an easy heel-and-toe. The synchro gearbox made for fast, smooth gear changes. With wishbone suspension at the front and fully independent suspension at the rear, the car was much more stable than previous models from the 1950s. The roar from the side exhaust was music to the ears of the driver, if somewhat deafening for the passenger.

For McQueen, the car was a dream. One touch of the accelerator on Mulholland Drive or Sunset, and he was Le Mans hero Mike Hawthorn ripping down the Mulsanne Straight. The best times were late at night or in the wee small hours—tearing it up on the road to Santa Monica. Local people say the police tried to stop him several times for speeding, but the *Green Rat* was always too fast for them. Neile found the car pretty sexy, too, with that plush cockpit just begging for acceleration. The XK-SS was the closest thing on Earth to a shooting star.

But deeply desirable though it was, the Jaguar was sold to another taker in December 1967. William F. Harrah, a serious collector of exceptional automobiles, bought it as an exhibit for his Harrah's Auto Museum in Nevada. A decade or so later, McQueen would buy it back, after more than two years of relentless, fierce wrangling. Fact was, his Jag had by that time become one of the most legendary cars of the postwar period.

In 1960, the McQueens moved into a big house with pool on Solar Drive, Hollywood. The house was immense and the swimming pool was a deep, limpid blue. Beside it was McQueen's private gym, where he worked out as religiously as he worked on his engines. On the other side of the garden was the garage. The couple loved their cars—and it certainly was a lineup to be proud of. Alongside the Jaguar XK-SS and the Lotus Eleven, there was Neile's Excalibur plus a Corvette Sting Ray and a Mustang. Later on when McQueen was married to Ali McGraw, there were his-and-her Mercedes: a 280 SE 3.5 Cabriolet for his wife, a luxurious 300 SEL 6.3 sedan for her husband. The 1970s added a Rolls-Royce Corniche Cabriolet bought on impulse in 1978. Before that, in 1976, McQueen's Porsche 911S was joined by an unthinkably powerful Porsche 930 Turbo—the car that fueled Chad McQueen's dreams once he got his driver's license. In the end it was sold to Dean Martin's son.

McQueen also had an impressive hoard of classic American cars: swank, grey 1949 Cadillac sedan; Hudson Wasp coupe and Hornet sedan, both 1951; 1931 Lincoln Club sedan; 1930 Cadillac V8 coupe; and several Packards including a Super 8 Convertible coupe, 1935 Chrysler Airflow and rare early 1950s Chrysler-engined Allard. Out at his ranches he kept a variety of pickups. And that's not counting the motorcycles of which McQueen had many. For competition, motocross and off-road use but also, of course, street motorcycles. These included a Triumph TR6 SC ISDT, Husqvarna 400 CR, Honda CR 250 Elsinore, Indian Chief, Norton, plus quite a few antique motorcycles (which he collected from the 1970s onward).

An impressive hoard to be sure, but not enough to persuade Hollywood that McQueen was a fully paid-up star. Missing from this collection of goodies were two iconic benchmarks of sixties style-consciousness: the Mini and the Ferrari. McQueen did, of course, eventually own both. The Mini was in fact a 1967 Mini Cooper S, probably acquired through his friendship with the Mini man himself, John Cooper. It was originally green with a white roof, but our man had it repainted brown and beige. A handsome wooden dash was crafted by Lee Brown's custom shop (at 5640 Hollywood Boulevard) and the interior was re-trimmed in light-brown vinyl by Tony Nancy. Other features included a single front-mounted fog light and a Vilem B. Haan leather-clad steering wheel with three silver anodized aluminum spokes. McQueen took delivery in late November 1967.

McQueen's other new wheels at around this time was a Ferrari. It was brown like the Mini, a lovely metallic brown with a light beige leather-upholstered interior. The car in question was a Berlinetta Lusso, one of Maranello's nicest Gran Turismo Coupes. It was the final model in the famed 250 GT series, and the most refined. "Lusso" is Italian for luxury. The car was in production for barely two years (1962-1964) and only 350 were built. The engine was the Colombo-designed 250 horsepower V-12, giving the Lusso a top speed of 150 miles per hour. The car had a short wheelbase chassis, similar to that of its sister cars, the 250 SWB Berlinetta and its starring racing counterpart, the 250 GTO.

This Ferrari was one of the very few sports cars that McQueen didn't buy for himself. It was a gift from his wife Neile for his 34th birthday, chassis Number 4891. She ordered it directly from Luigi Chinetti, Ferrari's then U.S. importer, and had it delivered to Mrs. McQueen by Santa Monica Ferrari concessionaire Otto Zipper Motors.

McQueen really loved that Ferrari. So sporty, yet so subtle and smooth. It was more of a Grand Tourer than a sports car, and really built to go the distance—a driving experience that fulfilled all expectations. A few years later, the McQueens acquired another Ferrari: a dark wine-colored 275 GTS/4 NART Spyder. This was one of those Italian muscle cars that turned heads in the street, same as lovely Vicky Anderson's Ferrari in Thomas Crown.

In face, it was in the filming of *The Thomas Crown Affair* that McQueen, like his character, first discovered the Ferrari 275 GTS/4 NART Spyder. Built for racing with the look of a stylish GT convertible and a truly stunning body—the Ferrari was irresistible. A smitten McQueen made inquiries and learned that this delectable number had been specially commissioned by Luigi Chinetti Ferrari's American importer, on behalf of the North American Racing Team (NART). The team was Luigi's baby, initially backed by wealthy gentlemen-racers who were good for the Ferrari brand image.

Ten NART Ferraris were built, each armed with a four-camshaft V12 engine that developed 330 horsepower. The one in the film was the first ever built, and one of only two with an alloy body. Alongside its glorious on-screen image, the car also boasted a racing record that did not fail to impress McQueen. He placed an order for the sixth car in the series, which was delivered in spring 1967. But something about the car was not quite right. Not the model itself or its performance, but the color. The blue was not deep enough. A purist to the last, McQueen once again got Lee Brown to do a custom paint job on the exterior. The seats were re-upholstered by Tony Nancy, the gas cap was replaced by a racing car's quick-fill cap and the rear lip spoiler was reshaped.

After all that work, and just days after McQueen collected it, the Ferrari was hit by a truck out on the Pacific Coast Highway. So ended a short but potentially beautiful relationship. The fabulous Ferrari was sold in 1971, but remains the stuff of car-buffs' dreams (fueled by every new showing of *The Thomas Crown Affair*).

Another iconic McQueen vehicle that had its debut in *The Thomas Crown Affair* was the Meyers Manx dune buggy. Built in 1964 by California designer Bruce Meyers, the Meyers Manx marked the beginning of a new vehicle craze. The original Meyers Manx was a short wheelbase VW Beetle-based dune buggy with a fiberglass body. It came in kit form and sold to some 5,000 buyers from 1964 to 1971. The Meyers Manx featured in several films, most famously in *The Thomas Crown Affair* where it was powered by a Chevy Corvair flat six, and not the usual VW flat four. There have been dozens of alternative designs since then, and as many companies making them. The one in the film found a home with McQueen who bought it for his own personal amusement.

By the end of the 1970s, McQueen was ready for a new toy. After tasting speed on terra firma, on two wheels and four, our sprightly forty-something took to the air. Flying became the new love in his life.

By July 1979, he was living in Santa Paula, California, with his new wife Barbara Minty, on a huge spread a few hundred miles from Los Angeles. It was there that he learned to fly and passed his private pilot exam. The more he flew, the more he loved airplanes, but not the luxurious private jets of rock stars and busy executives. No, what McQueen wanted was the wind in his hair, communion with nature as he left the Earth behind him. And so he started collecting vintage aircraft. The first was a dark blue Stearman Continental W670, which he registered as 3188, his inmate number back at reform school. Aviation for McQueen was a gateway to new sensations at a time when his body was battling disease. It was also a way of making new friends in his new somewhat rustic home region—a chance to mix with the kind of ordinary people he liked. He bought an airplane hangar on a Santa Paula airfield for his planes but also as a place to live from time to time, sharing the same corrugated-iron roof with his new toys. As soon as he passed his pilot's license, he bought a 1941 Boeing-Stearman PT-17 Kaydet Trainer, a military training plane recognizable at a glance by its bright yellow livery. Next, he bought one of six planes built in the 1930s for the pioneers of American airmail. With infinite patience, he restored the Pitcairn PA-8 Mailwing biplane, restoring it to its original glory in blue and white livery marked with the insignia of the U.S. Mail. He clearly took great pride in doing his bit to preserve his country's heritage.

Review the inventory of McQueen's machines, and you can see themes. You see personal preferences and you see an impulse to have it all. All of which serves as a moving testament to the man himself. His collection was not the stuff of overnight stars or the fleeting purchases of quick and easy money that fuels a moment of sensational buying power. McQueen was never ostentatious. The machines he chose were never picked for reasons of social status or to honor the conventions of his time. He chose them because there was something about each one that appealed to his sense of taste. Steve McQueen was one of those rare people with a sense of style that springs from life itself.

On location in Japan for the filming of Robert Wise's *The Sand Pebbles*, McQueen seizes the opportunity to take a Suzuki road racer for a spin through town. He received a Best Actor nomination in the Academy Awards for his performance in this film.

Opposite and above: McQueen and his mechanic discuss the tuning of his Jaguar XK-SS. Of all the speed machines he owned, this was certainly his favorite. Understandable, as there was something mythical about the XK-SS: only 16 were produced, and its 250-horsepower six-cylinder engine could propel the Jag to a top speed of 180 miles per hour with 0–60 miles per hour coming in just 4.7 seconds. Unbeatable performance for those times in any so-called "road" car.

Launched in 1957 with a catalog price of 6,900 Pounds Sterling, the Jaguar XK-SS is one of today's most collectable cars—valued at around five to six million dollars. It obviously helps that Steve McQueen was among the 16 lucky enough to own one.

McQueen in 1958, pointing to the red Scuderia Condor shield (the name of his first production company) he has just added to his newly acquired Jaguar XK-SS (D-Type chassis 569). The McQueens purchased it for $5,000 from then well-known radio broadcaster Bill Leyden (it was wife Neile who signed the check). The Jag at that point was white with a red interior, but McQueen soon had it repainted British Racing Green and reupholstered in black leather. He affectionately nicknamed the car *The Green Rat*.

Previous page: Ever on the lookout for a new acquisition—McQueen eyes up the Mercedes 300 SL Porter Special before testing it on the circuit.

Above and right: McQueen steps into the cockpit of his Lotus Eleven he bought in 1959. Light and powerful, the Eleven made a big impression in the 1100cc category at Le Mans in 1956 and 1957.

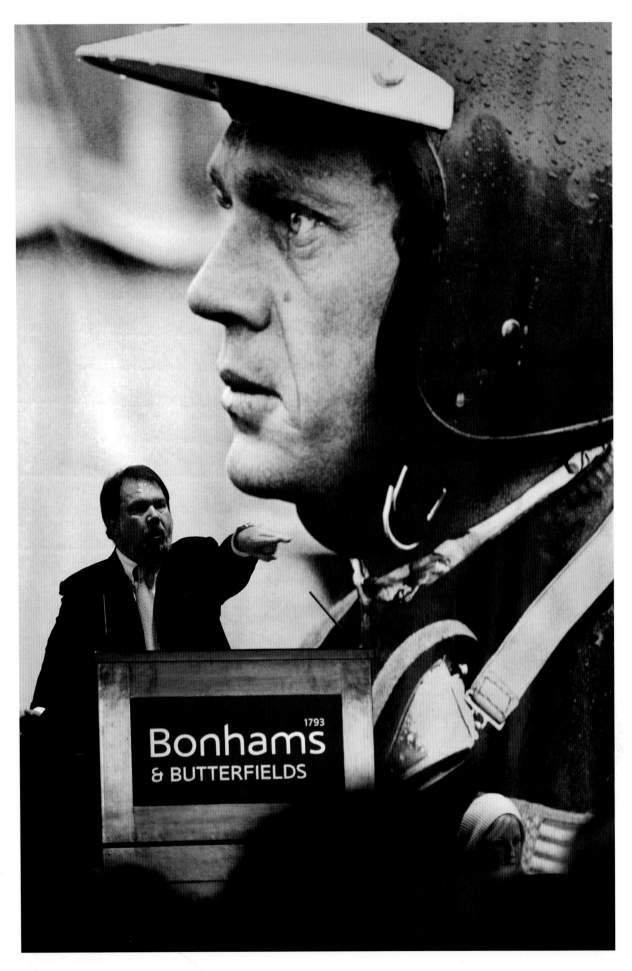

STEVE McQUEEN

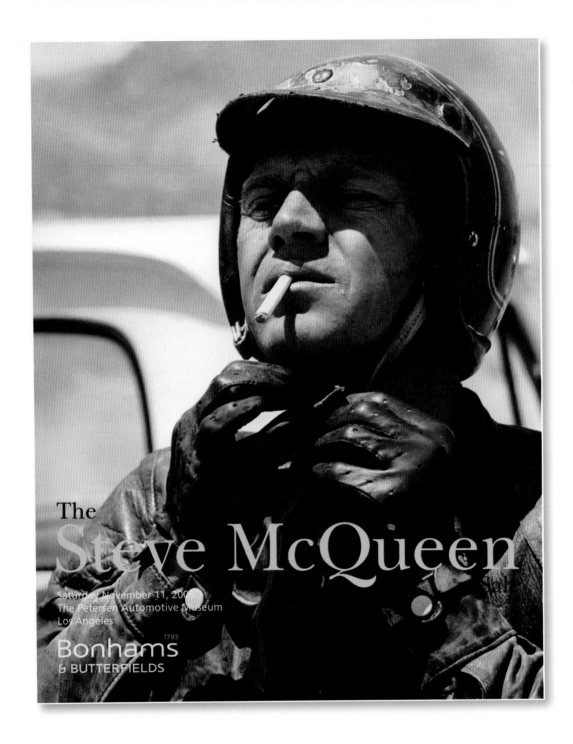

The
Steve McQueen
Sal

Saturday November 11, 200
The Petersen Automotive Museum
Los Angeles

Bonhams 1793
& BUTTERFIELDS

Preceding pages and above: In November 2006, Bonhams & Butterfields staged an auction sale of objects that had belonged to Steve McQueen. Among the furniture, clothing, glasses, credit cards, weapons, transistor radios, and vintage toys, the starring attractions were McQueen's collectible cars and motorcycles.

Right, top: Expected to fetch between $40,000 and $60,000, this sky blue 1958 GMC pickup (used by McQueen to drive around unnoticed) actually sold for $128,000.

Right, bottom: Christie's auction house sold McQueen's Ferrari 250 GT Berlinetta Lusso in August 2007. Expected to fetch between $800,000 and $1.2 million, it sold to a private buyer for a hefty $2.3 million, a record for this particular model.

Above: In November 2007, McQueen's motorcycles were featured among those offered for sale at Bonham & Butterfield's annual auction at the Petersen Automotive Museum, Los Angeles. This 100cc Kawasaki G31M, *Ringadingdoo*, was one of six machines supplied by the Japanese company for the filming of *Le Mans* to help McQueen move around the 8-mile-plus circuit. When shooting was done, McQueen kept this particular bike, which he had repainted orange. Expected to fetch between $18,000 and $25,000, *Ringadingdoo* more than doubled that figure at $55,500 dollars.

Left: Two motorcycles sold at Bonhams' 2006 Steve McQueen auction. Top: 1920 1000cc Indian Powerplus Daytona, sold for $150,000—$60,000 over the reserve. Below: 1929 Harley-Davidson Model B, sold for $37,000—twice the reserve.

In 1966, McQueen took his superb Ferrari 250 GT Berlinetta Lusso for an outing at Riverside Raceway. The machine was bought new, finished to McQueen's specifications, with a metallic brown exterior to match its beige leather interior.

Steve and wife Neile pose for the camera outside their Beverly Hills home, perched on the rear deck of their Ferrari 275 GTS Spyder.

Next page: The couple also owned an Excalibur, though it was Neile who used it on a daily basis.

LIFE

Conservatives Take G.O.P. Lead

THE GOLDWATER RUSH

STEVE McQUEEN — Problem kid becomes a star

THE STEVE McQUEENS OUT RIDING

JULY 12 · 1963 · 25¢

Left and above: McQueen and wife Neile. In 1963, the couple made the cover of *Life* magazine.

My thanks to Studio Gorne, especially Alexandre, for getting involved with this project and bringing out the best in these often legendary but frequently unseen images of Steve McQueen.

—YB Editions Publisher

Photogravure réalisée par

STUDIO Créa
GORNE
www.gorne.fr

5, place du Panthéon 75005 Paris
Tél. 01 44 41 65 00

ACKNOWLEDGEMENTS

Rémi Gammal, this book is for you. . . .

Pounding down the A13 Normandy Highway at 140 miles per hour in your snarling Coyote, with only your close-fitting shades and the car reflectors for company.

Or at the wheel of a Princess Mark IV, foot-to-floor . . . driving at 25 miles per hour on the bucolic lanes of Upper-Normandy.

Or flat-out in sixth at Nürburgring, Magny-Cours, Estoril, or Spa-Francorchamps.

Wherever you are, remember to ease off the accelerator in the bends and to take a break every 150 miles, if not sooner. You are dear to us.

Frédéric Brun

A special word of thanks to Jean-Christophe Giuseppi, Louis Galanos, Matthieu Lamoure, Pierre Novokoff, Iris Humel, and Cyril Pigot for their invaluable help with the photography research.

Also to Iannis Domon for letting me rummage through his collection of "forgotten" negatives and revive unpublished photographs just waiting to be restored, printed, and displayed for all to see. McQueen is well worth it. For his sake, my thanks.

Yann-Brice Dherbier

CREDITS